Charcuterie Boards Cookbook

Surprise and Delight with these Creative Charcuterie Board Recipes | Delicious, Mouthwatering, Beginner-Friendly Ideas to Wow Everyone

Mick Jarvis

TABLE OF CONTENTS

Introduction

What do we mean when we say "charcuterie"? Aside from being a great way to showcase and enjoy the incredible array of smoked, salted, and cured meats from the world of charcuterie, they are a perfect conversation starter and gathering place for guests. It has become so central to our get-togethers that we also include them in our chef business. When we prepare for events and celebrations, we always bring a charcuterie board to break the ice and get the conversation going. There is comfort and connection created when sharing thoughts and feelings over food.

While charcuterie is a French word, people across many cultures have been preserving meat for centuries. It was once a necessity to keep this precious commodity for a long time without spoiling, long before the invention of the refrigerator. This ancient style of preserving meats by drying and salting extended the life of meat during the heat of summer and kept it safe to eat over a long, cold winter. Charcuterie is the art of making meat products. The main types are sausages, hams, dry sausages, bacon, pâtés, terrines and galantines. Charcuterie is part of the preservation process by curing the meat and adding natural ingredients such as nitrates and nitrites. It's technically a subset of "cooking," but requires so many specialized processes that it technically becomes an art form in itself.

We believe in bringing people together over a memorable meal. It's a tradition in our home to gather every Sunday with family and friends, and one of the most important offerings we produce is a beautiful charcuterie board. The ritual is a natural extension of our Italian and Spanish heritages, with parents and grandparents who taught us about ingredients and flavors common on antipasto and tapas plates. Through this guide, you will learn how to make incredible charcuterie arrangements that will get your guests talking!

Breakfast recipes

1. Bacon Omelet

Prep Time: 15 mins

Cook it in: 15 mins

Servings: 2

Ingredients:

- 4 large eggs
- 1 tablespoon fresh chives, minced
- Salt and freshly ground black pepper, to taste
- 4 bacon slices
- 1 tablespoon unsalted butter
- 2 ounces cheddar cheese, shredded

Instructions:

1. In a bowl, add the eggs, chives, salt and black pepper and beat until well combined.

2. Heat a non-stick frying pan over medium-high heat and cook the bacon slices for about 8-10 minutes.

3. Place the bacon onto a paper towel-lined plate to drain. Then chop the bacon slices.

4. With paper towels, wipe out the frying pan.

5. In the same frying pan, melt the butter over medium-low heat and cook the egg mixture for about 2 minutes.

6. Carefully flip the omelet and top with chopped bacon.

7. Cook for 1-2 minutes or until desired doneness of eggs.

8. Remove from heat and immediately place the cheese in the center of the omelet.

9. Fold the edges of the omelet over cheese and cut into 2 portions.

10. Serve immediately.

Per serving:

Calories: 622

Fat: 49.3g

Saturated Fat: 20.7g

Trans Fat: 28.6g

Carbohydrates: 2g

Fiber: 0g

Sodium: 1700mg

Protein: 41.2g

2. Smoked Salmon Scramble

Prep Time: 10 mins

Cook it in: 5 mins

Servings: 6

Ingredients:

12 eggs

½ cup heavy cream

½ cup fresh chives, chopped

Salt and freshly ground black pepper, to taste

2 tablespoons butter

¼ pound sliced smoked salmon, chopped finely

Instructions:

1. In a bowl, add the eggs and cream and beat until well combined.
2. Add ¼ cup of the chives, salt and black pepper and stir to combine.
3. In a large non-stick skillet, melt the butter over medium heat.
4. Add the egg mixture and cook for about 2-3 minutes, stirring continuously with a wooden spoon.
5. Stir in the salmon and cook for about 1-2 minutes.
6. Serve hot with the garnishing of remaining chives.

Per serving:

Calories: 218

Fat: 17.1g

Saturated Fat: 7.7g

Trans Fat: 10g

Carbohydrates: 1.1g

Fiber: 0.1g

Sodium: 559mg

Protein: 14.9g

3. Beef Waffles

Prep Time: 10 mins

Cook it in: 12 mins

Servings: 4

Ingredients:

2 eggs, beaten

¾ cup cheddar cheese, shredded

2 cooked bacon slices, chopped

Instructions:

1. Preheat a mini waffle iron and then grease it.

2. In a bowl, place all the ingredients and mix until well combined.

3. Place ¼ of the mixture into preheated waffle iron and cook for about 2½-3 minutes or until golden brown.

4. Repeat with the remaining mixture.

5. Serve warm.

Per serving:

Calories: 128

Fat: 10.2g

Saturated Fat: 5.5g

Trans Fat: 4.7g

Carbohydrates: 0.4g

Fiber: 0g

Sodium: 379mg

Protein: 8.8g

4. Eggs in Bacon Cups

Prep Time: 10 mins

Cook it in: 20 mins

Servings: 6

Ingredients:

6 bacon slices

6 eggs

Salt and freshly ground black pepper, to taste

¼ cup cheddar cheese, shredded

2 tablespoons fresh chives, chopped

Instructions:

1. Preheat the oven to 400 degrees F.

2. Arrange the bacon slices into muffin cups, wrapping in a circle.

3. Bake for about 10 minutes.

4. Remove the muffin tin from the oven and discard any grease from cups.

5. Carefully crack 1 egg into each cups over bacon and sprinkle with salt, black pepper and cheddar cheese.

6. Bake for about 10 minutes more or until desired doneness of eggs.

7. Remove from the oven and set aside for about 2-3 minutes.

8. Run a knife around the edge of

each cup to loosen.

9. Transfer the bacon cups with eggs onto serving plates and serve with the garnishing of chives.

Per serving:

Calories: 237

Fat: 17.9g

Saturated Fat: 6.3g

Trans Fat: 11.6g

Carbohydrates: 0.9g

Fiber: 0g

Sodium: 780mg

Protein: 17.4g

5. Chicken & Bacon Waffles

Prep Time: 10 mins

Cook it in: 8 mins

Servings: 2

Ingredients:

1 egg, beaten

1/3 cup cooked chicken, chopped

1 cooked bacon slice, crumbled

1/3 cup Pepper Jack cheese, shredded

1 teaspoon powdered ranch dressing

Instructions:

1. Preheat a mini waffle iron and then grease it.

2. In a medium bowl, place all ingredients and with a fork, mix until well combined.

3. Place half of the mixture into preheated waffle iron and cook for about 3-4 minutes or until golden brown.

4. Repeat with the remaining mixture.

5. Serve warm.

Per serving:

Calories: 145

Fat: 9.4g

Saturated Fat: 4.6g

Trans Fat: 4.8g

Carbohydrates: 1g

Fiber: 0.1g

Sodium: 1200mg

Protein: 14.3g

6. Sausage & Bacon Rolls

Prep Time: 15 mins

Cook it in: 10 mins

Servings: 2

Ingredients:

4 gluten-free cooked breakfast sausages

4 eggs, beaten

2 cooked bacon slices

1/3 cup cheddar cheese, shredded

Instructions:

1. Heat a small non-stick frying pan over medium-low heat.
2. Add 2 beaten eggs and spread in an even layer.
3. Cover the pan and cook for about 2-3 minutes.
4. Sprinkle with half of the cheese and cook, covered, for about 1 minute.
5. Remove from the heat and place 2 breakfast sausages and 1 bacon slice in the center.
6. Carefully roll the egg wrap and transfer onto the serving plate.
7. Repeat with the remaining ingredients.
8. Cut each roll into slices and serve immediately.

Per serving:

Calories: 475

Fat: 32g

Saturated Fat: 11.2g

Trans Fat: 20.8g

Carbohydrates: 3.4g

Fiber: 0g

Sodium: 1300mg

Protein: 49.7g

7. Tuna Muffins

Prep Time: 10 mins

Cook it in: 30 mins

Servings: 3

Ingredients:

1 (7-ounce) can water-packed tuna, drained

3 ounces sharp cheddar cheese, shredded

1 tablespoon fresh parsley,

chopped

Salt and freshly ground black pepper, to taste

¼ cup mayonnaise

¼ cup sour cream

2 large eggs

¼ cup scallion, chopped

Instructions:

1. Preheat the oven to 350 degrees F. Grease 6 cups of a muffin tin.

2. In a bowl, add all the ingredients and mix until well combined.

3. Place the muffin mixture into the prepared muffin cups evenly.

4. Bake for about 25-30 minutes or until top becomes golden brown.

5. Remove the muffin tin from the oven and place onto a wire rack to cool for about 10 minutes.

6. Invert the muffins onto a platter and serve warm.

Per serving:

Calories: 449

Fat: 35.4g

Saturated Fat: 12.6g

Trans Fat: 22.8g

Carbohydrates: 2.1g

Fiber: 0.3g

Sodium: 438mg

Protein: 29.6g

8. Sausage Omelet

Prep Time: 15 mins

Cook it in: 40 mins

Servings: 6

Ingredients:

½ pound gluten-free sausage, casing removed and crumbled

8 large organic eggs

1 cup cheddar cheese, shredded

½ cup heavy whipping cream

Salt and freshly ground black pepper, to taste

Instructions:

1. Preheat the oven to 350 degrees F. Grease a 9x13-inch baking dish.

2. Heat a non-stick frying pan over medium heat and cook the sausage for about 8–10 minutes or until cooked through.

3. Meanwhile, in a bowl, add the remaining ingredients and beat

until well combined.

4. Remove from the heat and drain off the grease from the sausage completely.

5. Place the cooked sausage in the bottom of the prepared baking dish evenly and top with the egg mixture.

6. Bake for about 30 minutes or until eggs are completely set.

7. Remove from the oven and carefully transfer the omelet onto a cutting board.

8. Cut into desired-sized wedges

and serve.

Per serving:

Calories: 334

Fat: 27.3g

Saturated Fat: 11.8g

Trans Fat: 15.5g

Carbohydrates: 1.1g

Fiber: 0g

Sodium: 524mg

Protein: 20.6g

Basic and Simple Recipes

9. Jamón Experience

Prepare it in: *10 minutes*

Cook it in: *40 minutes*

Servings: *3*

Ingredients

- 1 cup Castelvetrano olives (or any mild green olive), not pitted
- 6 ounces jamón ibérico (or prosciutto), thinly sliced
- 4 ounces Manchego (or any mild sheep milk cheese), broken into rough pieces
- 1 baguette
- 2 tablespoons garlic-infused olive oil
- Sea salt

Instructions

1. Fill a small bowl with Castelvetrano olives and place it near the top right corner of the board.

2. Gently fold the jamón in wavy ribbons near the center top of the board.

3. Place the roughly broken pieces of Manchego below the jamón in the center of the board.

4. Tear the baguette in half. Leave one-half intact, and with a serrated knife slice open the other half.

5. Gently brush a small amount of olive oil inside the sliced baguette pieces, then sprinkle the oiled sides with sea salt. Brush one stroke of oil across the top of the uncut piece. Place the bread on the left side of the board.

6. **Drink pairing**: Manzanilla is a Spanish sherry best served chilled to accompany cured meat or seafood. It has a dry, fresh, and delicate palate of floral notes reminiscent of chamomile, almonds, and yeast. It's absolutely perfect with jamón and this tapas-style spread.

Per serving:

Calories: 145

Fat: 9.4g

Saturated Fat: 4.6g

Trans Fat: 4.8g

Carbohydrates: 1g

Fiber: 0.1g

Sodium: 1200mg

Protein: 14.3g

10. Cheeseburger Dip

Prepare it in: *10 minutes*

Cook it in: *30 minutes*

Servings: *4*

Ingredients

- 2 tablespoons olive oil
- ½ pound lean ground beef
- Salt and pepper to taste
- 1 cup sour cream
- 2 cups shredded provolone cheese
- 1 teaspoon freshly chopped thyme
- 1 teaspoon dried oregano
- ½ cup cream cheese
- ½ cup heavy cream

Instructions

1. Warm the olive oil in a pan.
2. Add the ground beef and cook for 10 minutes.
3. Stir in the sour cream, cheese, thyme, oregano, and cream cheese.
4. Pour in the heavy cream and transfer the mixture to a 9×13 baking dish.
5. Cook in a preheated oven at 350°F (180°C) for about 15–20 minutes.
6. Serve with your favorite tortilla chips.

Per serving:

Calories 137,

Fat 5.7,

Fiber 10.9,

Carbs 21.2,

Protein 4.2

11. Kids in Bologna

Prepare it in: *10 minutes*

Cook it in: *40 minutes*

Servings: *3*

Ingredients

- 6 grissini sticks
- A small bundle of fresh basil leaves
- 2 tablespoons balsamic reduction or glaze
- 1 cup cherry tomatoes
- 8 ounces fresh Mozzarella bocconcini (or fresh mozzarella cut into bite-size pieces)
- 4 ounces mortadella (or any mild deli meat), thinly sliced

Instructions

1. Place the grissini in a glass sticking straight up and barely offset from the center of the board.

2. At the base of the grissini glass, place the bundle of basil and a mini bowl of balsamic reduction.

3. Visually divide the board into thirds (imagine drawing a peace sign on the board), and place the cherry tomatoes, bocconcini, and mortadella each in its own section.

4. **Drink pairing**: Chocolate egg cream—a delicious and kid-friendly blend of chocolate syrup, milk, and seltzer—is a classic of Italian American soda shops in New York City. For each serving, blend ½ cup whole milk and ¼ cup chocolate syrup together.

5. If you have an immersion blender or high-speed blender, you can get that frothy texture and soda shop experience. Pour the chocolate milk into a tall glass and top with seltzer. Finish with a cute straw and serve.

Pro tip: *Chill the glasses in the freezer for a frosty cold treat.*

Per serving:

Calories: 145

Fat: 9.4g

Saturated Fat: 4.6g

Trans Fat: 4.8g

Carbohydrates: 1g

Fiber: 0.1g

Sodium: 1200mg

Protein: 14.3g

12. Salami Keto Lovers

Prepare it in: *10 minutes*

Cook it in: *45 minutes*

Servings: *2*

Ingredients

- 1 cup fresh garlic ricotta (see Variation)
- 4 Mini Chaffles
- Extra-virgin olive oil, for drizzling
- Freshly ground black pepper
- 3 ounces Salami Picante, casing removed, thinly sliced
- 3 ounces Creminelli Whiskey Salami Minis (or any mild salami)
- You will also need: a board, a small bowl, a small spoon, a small upright dish or glass

Instructions

1. Prepare the fresh garlic ricotta and chaffles according to the recipes. The ricotta can be prepared up to a week ahead of time, but the chaffles are best served warm or at room temperature.

2. Place the ricotta in a small bowl with a spoon, near the center of the board but slightly to the left. Drizzle it with olive oil and grind some pepper over the top.

3. Arrange the chaffles off to the right side of the ricotta, stacking and shingling them to look pretty.

4. Arrange the salami slices below the ricotta.

5. Put the mini salami sticks in a small upright dish or glass near the top left side of the board.

Drink pairing: Keeping with the keto theme, pair this spread with some replenishing electrolyte water. Packed with sodium, potassium, and magnesium, this is a must for keto dieters (who tend to lose electrolytes due to water loss) and a great pick-me-up for anybody who wants to feel hydrated and refreshed. In a pitcher, combine 3 cups of filtered water, ¼ teaspoon sea salt, 130 mg potassium powder, and 45 mg magnesium powder. Squeeze in the juice of half a lemon and stir well to mix.

Per serving:

Calories: 121

Fat: 4.4g

Saturated Fat: 4.7g

Trans Fat: 4.8g

Carbohydrates: 3g

Fiber: 0.1g

Sodium: 1270mg

Protein: 16.3g

13. Summer Berry Fields

Prepare it in*: 10 minutes*

Cook it in*: 3 hours minutes*

Servings*: 3*

Ingredients

- 1 cup Oven-Dried Strawberries
- 4 ounces pancetta, thinly sliced
- 1 tablespoon olive oil
- 1 tablespoon granulated sugar
- 2 teaspoons lemon juice

- ½ cup blackberries
- 1 cup raspberries
- 4 thick slices of brioche
- 2 tablespoons unsalted butter
- Pinch ground cinnamon
- Pinch confectioners' sugar
- 8 ounces mascarpone cheese
- 2 tablespoons honey
- You will also need: a platter, a small bowl, a small spoon, a butter knife, a small jar, a honey wand

Instructions

1. Prepare the oven-dried strawberries according to the recipe. The strawberries can be prepared up to 2 weeks ahead of time.

2. Heat a skillet over high heat. Add the pancetta and drizzle with the olive oil. Sauté the pancetta for 6 to 8 minutes, until it crisps up like cooked bacon. Set aside.

3. In a medium bowl, mix the granulated sugar and lemon juice. Add the blackberries and

raspberries, and gently toss to coat them with the mixture. Set aside to steep for 5 minutes.

4. Toast the brioche slices and spread with the butter. Place the brioche along the left side of the board, from the top to just below the center. Top the brioche with the macerated raspberries and blackberries. Finish with a sprinkling of cinnamon and confectioners' sugar.

5. Spoon the mascarpone into a heap near the lower right corner of the brioche.

6. Place the crispy pancetta on the top right corner of the board.

7. Pile the oven-dried strawberries in a small bowl, and place it in the bottom left corner with a small serving spoon next to it.

8. Just above or next to the strawberries, place the honey in a small jar with a honey wand.

Drink pairing: Some French champagne is a great accompaniment to this board. If you are celebrating and want to splurge, Dom Pérignon is the ultimate pairing, but if you'd like to go with something lower-key but still elegant, fresh, and light, an authentic Brut such as Canard-Duchêne is great, too.

Per serving:

Calories: 231

Fat: 8.4g

Saturated Fat: 4.6g

Trans Fat: 5.8g

Carbohydrates: 6g

Fiber: 0.1g

Sodium: 1300mg

Protein: 18.3g

14. Cherries and Almonds

Prepare it in: *10 minutes*

Cook it in: *45 minutes*

Servings: *3*

Ingredients

- ½ cup Pecan Granola
- 2 cups plain Greek yogurt
- 4 ounces bresaola (or lonzino), thinly sliced
- 2 cups cherries
- 1 cup Marcona almonds (or any salted blanched almonds)
- 5 to 6 ounces honeycomb squares
- You will also need: a board, 2 small bowls, 2 spoons, a small knife

Instructions

1. Prepare the pecan granola according to the recipe. The granola can be prepared up to a month ahead of time.
2. Divide the Greek yogurt into two small bowls and top each with half of the pecan granola. Set the bowls side by side in the center of a large board with a spoon in each bowl.
3. In the top right corner, arrange the bresaola.
4. In the bottom left corner, add the cherries.
5. Above the cherries, pile the Marcona almonds.
6. On the bottom right, add the honeycomb squares, with a small knife.

Drink pairing: The sweetness and textures of this board make an exciting pairing with kriek, a hoppy, cherry-flavored beer from Belgium typically made with sour cherries. American brewery Strange Craft Beer Company makes a great one, but for the real deal, try Belgium's Lindemans Brewery kriek lambic beer.

Per serving:

Calories: 245

Fat: 7.4g

Saturated Fat: 6.6g

Trans Fat: 7.8g

Carbohydrates: 7g

Fiber: 0.1g

Sodium: 1450mg

Protein: 17.3g

15. Barbecue Meatloaf

*Prepare & **Cook it in***: *45 mins*

Servings: *4*

Ingredients

- 1 lb 93% lean ground beef
- 1/2 cup barbecue sauce, divided
- 1/4 cup frozen chopped onions, pressed dry
- 1/4 cup Italian seasoned breadcrumbs
- 2 large egg whites

Cooking Instructions

1. Preheat the oven at 190C/375F.
2. In a large bowl, mix together the meat, egg whites, onion, 1/4 cup barbecue sauce, breadcrumbs, &seasons of your liking and stir well.
3. Form the mixture into a loaf pan. Spread the leftover barbecue sauce at the top of the loaf.
4. Bake at 190C/375F until it reaches your desired doneness, approximately 40 to 50 minutes.

Per serving:

Calories: 145

Fat: 9.4g

Saturated Fat: 4.6g

Trans Fat: 4.8g

Carbohydrates: 1g

Fiber: 0.1g

Sodium: 1200mg

Protein: 14.3g

16. Quick & Easy BBQ Meatloaf

*Prepare & **Cook it in***: *50 mins*

Servings: *4*

Ingredients

- 1 Lb Ground Beef
- 1/2 Cup Barbecue Sauce
- 1/2 Cup Quick Oats, Uncooked
- 1/2 Cup Onion, Chopped Finely
- 1 Egg, Beaten

Cooking Instructions

1. Mix together everything but don't mix barbecue sauce (approximately 1/4 cup).
2. Form the mixture into a loaf and then in a baking dish (12x8inch).

3. Bake at 190C/375F until cooked through, approximately 50 mins. Before slicing, let the loaf to stand approximately 5 minutes. Top with leftover barbecue sauce.

Per serving:

Calories: 145

Fat: 9.4g

Saturated Fat: 4.6g

Trans Fat: 4.8g

Carbohydrates: 1g

Fiber: 0.1g

Sodium: 1200mg

Protein: 14.3g

17. Cranberry & Turkey Meatloaf

*Prepare & **Cook it in**: 1hr & 5 mins*

Servings: *6*

Ingredients

- 1 1/2 Lbs Ground Turkey
- 1 (120 G) Box Turkey Stuffing Mix
- 2 Eggs
- 1/3 Cup Milk Or 1/3 Cup Water
- 1/2 Cup Onion, Diced
- 1/2 Cup Celery, Diced
- 1/2 Cup Dried Cranberries

Cooking Instructions

1. In a large bowl, mix together everything and combine well.
2. Transfer the mixture to a loaf pan (already greased).
3. Bake uncovered in a preheated oven at 350 F/175C approximately an hour.
4. Remove the loaf from the heat & before slicing, allow it to rest approximately 10 minutes at room temperature.

Per serving:

Calories: 449

Fat: 35.4g

Saturated Fat: 12.6g

Trans Fat: 22.8g

Carbohydrates: 2.1g

Fiber: 0.3g

Sodium: 438mg

Protein: 29.6g

18. Cajun Meatloaf

*Prepare & **Cook it in**: 1hr & 20 mins*

Servings: *8*

Ingredients

- 1 Tablespoon Vegetable Oil
- 2 Garlic Cloves, Finely Chopped
- 1 Onion, Diced
- 1 Carrot, Diced
- 1/2 Cup Red Bell Pepper, Diced
- 1 Tablespoon Cajun Seasoning
- 1/2 Teaspoon Salt
- 1/2 Teaspoon Ground Black Pepper
- 1/2 Cup Corn Kernel
- 1 Egg, Beaten
- 1 1/2 Cups Corn Chips, Roughly Crushed
- 1/2 Cup Salsa
- 1/4 Cup Water
- 1 Lb Lean Ground Beef
- 1 Lb Ground Lean Pork
- 1/2 Cup Cheddar Cheese, Grated
- 2 Tablespoons Fresh Parsley, Chopped

Cooking Instructions

1. Heat oil on medium heat settings in a large skillet. Add Cajun seasoning, onion, garlic, red bell pepper, carrot, pepper and salt. Cook, until onion has softened, approximately 5 minutes, stirring occasionally. Add corn & continue cooking for 2 more minutes. Let the mixture to cool for some time.

2. Mix corn chips, egg, water, salsa, mixture of veggies & pork and beef in a big bowl. Spoon this mixture on a baking sheet with foil paper &shape in a 9x5" loaf. Cook in oven (preheated) at 175C/350 F approximately 80 mins. Sprinkle cheddar cheese over the top & continue cooking until internal temperature displays 170F, approximately 10 more minutes. Let the meatloaf to stand approximately 5 mins. Drain off meatloaf fat then sprinkle parsley over it.

Per serving:

Calories: 145

Fat: 9.4g

Saturated Fat: 4.6g

Trans Fat: 4.8g

Carbohydrates: 1g

Fiber: 0.1g

Sodium: 1200mg

Protein: 14.3g

19. Taco Meatloaf

*Prepare & **Cook it in**: 1hr & 5 mins*

Servings: *6*

Ingredients

- 1 1/2 Lbs Ground Beef
- 1 Cup Tortilla Chips Or 1 Cup Corn Chips, Crushed
- 1/3 Cup Salsa Or 1/3 Cup Taco Sauce
- 1 Tablespoon Taco Seasoning
- 1 Egg, Beaten
- 1 Cup Cheddar Cheese, Shredded

Cooking Instructions

1. Use your hands to mix everything in a large bowl.
2. Bake at 175C/350 F approximately an hour in a loaf pan.

3. Drain off fat &bake for one or two more minutes.

Per serving:

Calories: 145

Fat: 9.4g

Saturated Fat: 4.6g

Trans Fat: 4.8g

Carbohydrates: 1g

Fiber: 0.1g

Sodium: 1200mg

Protein: 14.3g

20. Gyro Loaf With Tsatziki Sauce

*Prepare & **Cook it in**: 2hr & 20 mins*

Servings: *8*

Ingredients

FOR GYRO LOAF

- 1 Lb Ground Lamb
- 1 Lb Ground Beef
- 1 Teaspoon Oregano
- 1 1/2 Tablespoons Onion Powder
- 1 Tablespoon Garlic Powder
- 3/4 Tablespoon Ground Pepper

- 1 Teaspoon Thyme
- 3/4 Teaspoon Salt
- 1/8 Teaspoon Cinnamon
- 1/8 Teaspoon Allspice

TSATZIKI SAUCE

- 1 Cup Sour Cream
- 1 Medium Cucumber, Grated & Squeezed Dry
- 1/2 Teaspoon Garlic Powder
- 1/2 Teaspoon Salt
- 1 Tablespoon Parsley
- 1/4 Teaspoon Dill

Cooking Instructions

1. Mix together the meat loaf ingredients &shape the mixture into a loaf (freeform) in a baking pan.
2. Bake at 190C/375F approximately 75 mins.
3. Slice the loaf as thin as possible, once the loaf has cooled at room temperature (maximum of ¼").
4. Serve it at room temperature or warm.
5. You can serve this meatloaf with pitas, tortillas or flatbreads with tomato, lettuce, feta cheese, Tsatziki Sauce &black olives or with a potato salad, Greek salad, or pasta salad.

Per serving:

Calories: 145

Fat: 9.4g

Saturated Fat: 4.6g

Trans Fat: 4.8g

Carbohydrates: 1g

Fiber: 0.1g

Sodium: 1200mg

Protein: 14.3g

21. Cracker Barrel Meatloaf

*Prepare & **Cook it in**: 1hr & 5 mins*

***Servings**: 9*

Ingredients

- 2 Eggs
- 2/3 Cup Milk
- 32 Ritz Crackers, Crushed
- 1/2 Cup Chopped Onion
- 4 Ounces Shredded Sharp Cheddar Cheese

- 1 Teaspoon Salt
- 1/4 Teaspoon Pepper
- 1 1/2 Lbs Ground Beef
- 1/2 Cup Ketchup
- 1/2 Cup Brown Sugar
- 1 Teaspoon Mustard

Cooking Instructions

1. Preheat your oven at 350F/175C.

2. Beat the eggs in a large bowl and add crackers and milk. Stir in cheese and onion and then add the ground beef. Combine the ingredients well and shape the mixture into a loaf.

3. Bake at 175C/350 F approximately 45 mins.

4. To make topping, combine brown sugar, mustard and ketchup. After half an hour of baking, spoon half of the topping over the meatloaf. Return the loaf to oven and bake approximately 10 mins more. Spoon the leftover topping over the meatloaf and return it to the oven &bake approximately 5mins more.

Per serving:

Calories: 145

Fat: 9.4g

Saturated Fat: 4.6g

Trans Fat: 4.8g

Carbohydrates: 1g

Fiber: 0.1g

Sodium: 1200mg

Protein: 14.3g

22. Turkey Meatloaf

Prepare & ***Cook it in****: 1hr & 20 mins*

Servings: *10*

Ingredients

- 1 Medium Onion, Finely Chopped
- 1 Tablespoon Canola Oil
- 2 Eggs
- 1/2 Cup 2% Low-Fat Milk
- 2 Teaspoons Lemon Juice
- 1 Teaspoon Salt
- 1 Teaspoon Dried Basil
- 1/2 Teaspoon Dried Oregano
- 1/2 Teaspoon Pepper
- 2 Cups Whole Wheat Bread

Crumbs, Soft

- 1 (10 Ounce) Package Frozen Spinach, Thawed And Squeezed Dry
- 2 1/2 Lbs Lean Ground Turkey
- 1/2 Cup Salsa
- 1 Tablespoon Butter

Cooking Instructions

1. Heat oil in a skillet& sauté the onion until tender; keep it aside.

2. Combine the lemon juice, milk, eggs, basil, salt, pepper and oregano in a large bowl. Add the reserved onion, bread crumbs and spinach; stir to combine well. Crumble turkey over the mixture &mix until well blended.

3. Shape the mixture into a loaf (12x5-inch); place in a baking dish (13x9x2-inch) coated with cooking spray (non-sticking).Spoon salsa at the top of the loaf.

4. Bake at 175C/350F approximately half an hour, uncovered. Drizzle butter; bake until a meat thermometer reflects 165 F, for half an hour more.

Per serving:

Calories: 145

Fat: 9.4g

Saturated Fat: 4.6g

Trans Fat: 4.8g

Carbohydrates: 1g

Fiber: 0.1g

Sodium: 1200mg

Protein: 14.3g

23. Easy Pleasing Meatloaf

*Prepare & **Cook it in**: 1hr & 20 mins*

***Servings:** 8*

Ingredients

- 1 Cup Water
- 2 Lbs Lean Ground Beef
- 1/2 Cup Onion, Finely Diced
- 1 (6 1/4 Ounce) Package Stove Top Stuffing Mix
- 2 Eggs
- 1/2 Cup Ketchup, Divided

Cooking Instructions

1. In A Large Bowl, Combine Everything Together But Keep 1/4 Cup Of Ketchup For Later Use.

2. Shape The Mixture To Loaf.

3. Place The Loaf In A Baking Dish (9x13 Inch).

4. Top The Loaf With The Leftover Ketchup.

5. Bake At 375 F/190C Approximately An Hour.

- turkey.

  Turkey Meatloaf

  Prepare & **Cook it in***: 1hr & 10 mins*

  Servings: *4*

  Ingredients

- 1 Lb Ground Turkey Breast
- 1/3 Cup Quick-Cooking Oats
- 1/4 Cup Nonfat Milk
- 1 Egg, Beaten
- 1/3 Cup Chili Sauce
- 1 Small Onion, Finely Chopped
- 1 Small Red Pepper, Finely Chopped
- 1 Tablespoon Worcestershire Sauce
- Salt And Pepper
- Ketchup

Cooking Instructions

1. Mix the milk and oats together in a small bowl and let the oats absorb the milk approximately 10 minutes.

2. In a large bowl, combine together everything (don't add the ketchup) and absorbed oats.

3. Using large fork, combine everything and mix well.

4. Using cooking spray, spray a baking pan (9x13 inch).

5. Shape the mixture into loaf& brush it with ketchup.

6. Bake at 175C/350 F approximately 50 mins. Serve warm and enjoy.

Per serving:

Calories: 145

Fat: 9.4g

Saturated Fat: 4.6g

Trans Fat: 4.8g

31

Carbohydrates: 1g

Fiber: 0.1g

Sodium: 1200mg

Protein: 14.3g

24. Meatloaf Muffins

*Prepare & **Cook it in**: 45 mins*

Servings: *8*

Ingredients

- 1 (6 Ounce) Box Stove Top Stuffing Mix
- 2 Eggs
- 1 Cup Water
- 2 Lbs Ground Beef Or 2 Lbs Turkey

Cooking Instructions

1. Mix everything together in a large bowl.
2. Use cooking spray to spray the muffin tins, esp.for the turkey.
3. Fill the muffins tins till top.
4. Bake at 175C/350F approximately half an hour.

Per serving:

Calories: 145

Fat: 9.4g

Saturated Fat: 4.6g

Trans Fat: 4.8g

Carbohydrates: 1g

Fiber: 0.1g

Sodium: 1200mg

Protein: 14.3g

25. Autumn Meatloaf

*Prepare & **Cook it in**: 1hr & 15 mins*

Servings: *12*

Ingredients

- 2 Lbs Ground Turkey
- 1 (10 Ounce) Package Frozen Chopped Spinach (Thawed, Drained And Squeeze Dry)
- 1 Cup Cheddar Cheese, Shredded
- 1/2 Cup Mushroom, Finely Chopped (Optional)
- 1/2 Cup Red Onion, Chopped Fine
- 4 Garlic Cloves, Chopped
- 1 (1 1/4 Ounce) Envelope Onion Soup Mix

- 2 Large Eggs, Beaten
- 1/2 Cup Plain Breadcrumbs
- 2 Tablespoons Prepared Yellow Mustard
- 1 Tablespoon Worcestershire Sauce
- 1/2 Teaspoon Poultry Seasoning
- 1/2 Teaspoon Black Pepper
- 2 Cups Tomato Ketchup (Optional)

Cooking Instructions

1. Mix everything together until well combined. Place the mixture into a loaf pan, large. If desired, spread ketchup at the top of the mixture.
2. Preheat the oven at 350F/175C &bake until internal temperature displays 165F, approximately an hour. Let stand, covered approximately 10 minutes to finish cooking and to set the meatloaf (final temperature should reflect 170F).
3. Remove the loaf from the pan and place on a serving platter.

Per serving:

Calories: 145

Fat: 9.4g

Saturated Fat: 4.6g

Trans Fat: 4.8g

Carbohydrates: 1g

Fiber: 0.1g

Sodium: 1200mg

Protein: 14.3g

26. Crock Pot Meatloaf

*Prepare & **Cook it in**: 8hrs & 15 mins*

***Servings:** 4*

Ingredients

- 1 Egg
- 1/4 Cup Milk
- 2 Slices Bread, Cubed Day Old
- 1/4onion, Finely Chopped
- 2 Tablespoons Finely Chopped Green Peppers
- 1 Teaspoon Salt
- 1/4 Teaspoon Pepper
- 1 1/2 Lbs Lean Ground Beef
- 1/4 Cup Ketchup

- 8 Medium Carrots, Peeled And Cut In 1 Inch Chunks
- 8 Small Red Potatoes

Cooking Instructions:

1. Beat egg &milk in a medium size bowl.
2. Stir in green pepper, onion, bread cubes, pepper and salt.
3. Put the pieces of beef in the mixture & combine well.
4. Form into a round loaf.
5. Place the loaf in a Crock Pot (5 qt).
6. Spread the ketchup over the top of the loaf.
7. Place carrots nearby the loaf in the Crockpot.
8. Peel a strip nearby every potato & arrange potatoes over the carrots.
9. Cover; cook on high settings approximately an hour. Decrease the heat to LOW settings. Cover; cook on low settings until vegetables are tender, and meat is no longer pink, approximately 7 to 8 hours.

Per serving:

Calories: 145

Fat: 9.4g

Saturated Fat: 4.6g

Trans Fat: 4.8g

Carbohydrates: 1g

Fiber: 0.1g

Sodium: 1200mg

Protein: 14.3g

27. Quaker Oats Meatloaf

*Prepare & **Cook it in**: 1hr & 15 mins*

***Servings:** 6*

Ingredients

- 2 Lbs Ground Beef
- 1 Cup Tomato Sauce Or 1 Cup Ketchup Or 1 Cup Salsa
- 3/4 Cup Quaker Oats
- 1/2 Cup Chopped Onion
- 1 Large Egg, Beaten
- 1 Tablespoon Soy Sauce Or 1 Tablespoon Worcestershire

Sauce

- Salt And Pepper

Cooking Instructions

1. Preheat your oven at 350F/175C and mix everything together. Shape the mixture into loaf and put in loaf pan &bake approximately an hour.

2. Drain the excess fat off from the loaf and add 2 eggs and 2/3 cup milk and bake for some more time.

Per serving:

Calories: 425

Fat: 5.4g

Saturated Fat: 4.6g

Trans Fat: 4.8g

Carbohydrates: 25g

Fiber: 0.1g

Sodium: 1200mg

Protein: 14.3g

28. Easy And Tasty Meatloaf

*Prepare & **Cook it in**: 55 mins*

***Servings:** 7*

Ingredients

- 1 Lb Ground Beef
- 2 Tablespoons Dry Onion Soup Mix
- 1 (5 Ounce) Can Evaporated Milk (2/3 Cup)
- 2 Tablespoons Ketchup
- 2 Tablespoons Firmly Packed Brown Sugar
- 1 Teaspoon Mustard

Cooking Instructions

1. Preheat your oven at 350 F/175C.

2. Combine beef, onion soup mix & evaporated milk in loaf pan (8x4 Inch); mix well. Press evenly in the pan.

3. In a small bowl, mix the ketchup, mustard, and brown sugar together and spoon over the mixture.

4. Bake approximately 45 mins.

5. Lift the meat loaf from the pan to a serving plate using spatulas. Serve warm & enjoy!

Per serving:

Calories: 145

Fat: 9.4g

Saturated Fat: 4.6g

Trans Fat: 4.8g

Carbohydrates: 1g

Fiber: 0.1g

Sodium: 1200mg

Protein: 14.3g

29. Salsa Meatloaf (OAMC)

*Prepare & **Cook it in**: 50 mins*

Servings: *1*

Ingredients For Loaf

- 1 Lb Ground Beef
- 3/4 Cup Breadcrumbs Or 3/4 Cup Cracker Crumbs Or 3/4 Cup Oatmeal
- 1 Small Onion, Diced
- 1 Tablespoon Worcestershire Sauce
- 1/2 Package Dry Onion Soup Mix
- 1 Egg
- 1 Teaspoon Garlic
- 1/2 Teaspoon Pepper
- 3/4 Cup Salsa

For Sauce

- 3/4 Cup Salsa
- 1 Teaspoon Brown Sugar
- 1 Teaspoon Chili Powder
- 2 Tablespoons Ketchup

Cooking Instructions

1. For loaf, mix the loaf ingredients together &place the mixture in a loaf pan.
2. Bake at 175C/350 F until almost done, approximately 45 minutes.
3. Top the loaf with sauce &bake 10 to 15 more minutes.
4. For OAMC: Complete the 1 & 2 step but bake until done. Defrost the mixture overnight, top it with sauce &then bake at 175C/350 F until sauce bubbles, approximately 20 minutes.

Per serving:

Calories: 145

Fat: 9.4g

Saturated Fat: 4.6g

Trans Fat: 4.8g

Carbohydrates: 1g

Fiber: 0.1g

Sodium: 1200mg

Protein: 14.3g

30. Ground Beef Meatloaf

Prepare & ***Cook it in****: 1 hr& 40 mins*

Servings: *6*

Ingredients

- 1 1/2 Lbs Ground Beef
- 1 Cup Cracker Crumb
- 1 1/4 Teaspoons Salt
- 1/4 Teaspoon Pepper
- 1 Large Egg, Beaten
- 1 Medium Onion, Chopped
- 1/2 Cup Tomato Sauce

For Topping

- 3/4 cup ketchup
- 2 tablespoons firmly packed brown sugar
- 1 cup water
- 2 tablespoons mustard
- 2 tablespoons vinegar

Cooking Instructions

1. Preheat the oven at 325 F/160C.
2. Mix together the cracker crumbs, ground beef, pepper, salt, tomato sauce, onion and egg in a large mixing bowl.
3. Mix very lightly.
4. Shape the mixture into loaf &place it in a baking dish.
5. Combine ketchup, water, brown sugar, vinegar and mustard in a small mixing bowl.
6. Brush this mixture on top of the loaf.
7. Arrange the meat loaf in an oven &bake basting occasionally with sauce, approximately 75 mins.

Per serving:

Calories: 145

Fat: 9.4g

Saturated Fat: 4.6g

Trans Fat: 4.8g

Carbohydrates: 1g

Fiber: 0.1g

Sodium: 1200mg

Protein: 14.3g

31. Cottage Cheese Roast

*Prepare & **Cook it in**: 1 hr& 20 mins*

Servings: *8*

Ingredients

- 1 (16 Ounce) Carton Cottage Cheese
- 4 Eggs, Beaten
- 1/4 Cup Vegetable Oil
- 1 (1 Ounce) Envelope Dry Onion Soup Mix
- 1 Cup Finely Chopped Walnuts
- 1 1/2-2 1/2 Cups Corn Flakes
- 1/4 Cup Chopped Onion

Cooking Instructions

1. Preheat the oven at 175 C/350 F and grease a loaf pan.
2. Mix together the eggs, walnuts, cottage cheese, soup mix, vegetable oil, onion and cereal in a large bowl.
3. Spoon the mixture into the prepared pan and bake approximately 75 mins.

4. Allow the 'roasted loaf' to rest approximately 10 mins; turn out the loaf onto a serving platter.

Delicious Beef Meatloaf

*Prepare & **Cook it in**: 1 hr& 20 mins*

Servings: *6*

Ingredients

- 2/3 Cup Evaporated Milk, Undiluted (Pet Brand Preferred)
- 1 Egg
- 1 Cup Cracker Crumb
- 1 1/2 Lbs Ground Beef
- 1/2 Cup Chopped Onion
- 1 1/2 Teaspoons Salt
- 1 Teaspoon Dry Mustard

Cooking Instructions

1. Mix the ingredients as per the given order and press into a greased loaf pan (8x5x3 inch).
2. Bake the mixture in oven at 175C/350F approximately an hour.
3. Before slicing, let the meat loaf to stand approximately 5 to 10 minutes.

Per serving:

Calories: 145

Fat: 9.4g

Saturated Fat: 4.6g

Trans Fat: 4.8g

Carbohydrates: 1g

Fiber: 0.1g

Sodium: 1200mg

Protein: 14.3g

32. Italian Meatloaf

Prepare & ***Cook it in****: 1 hr& 45 mins*

Servings: *8*

Ingredients

- 3 Cups Soft Breadcrumbs
- 3/4 Cup Milk
- 2 Teaspoons Salt
- 1/4 Teaspoon Pepper
- 1/2 Teaspoon Thyme
- 3/4 Teaspoon Basil
- 1 (8 Ounce) Can Tomato Sauce
- 1/2 Cup Onion, Chopped
- 2 Tablespoons Butter
- 2 Lbs Lean Ground Beef

- 1 Cup Mozzarella Cheese, Shredded

Cooking Instructions

1. Let the bread to soak the milk.
2. Add thyme, pepper, salt, 1/4 cup tomato sauce, 1/2 tsp basil; stir & break up the bread cubes, using fork.
3. Sauté onions in butter until soft, approximately 5 minutes and then add onions to the bread mixture.
4. Lightly mix the ingredients using fork.
5. Add ground beef to the mixture & if required, mix beef with the mixture using your hands.
6. Turn the mixture into a loaf pan& bake at 175C/350F approximately an hour; then drain the excess fat.
7. Turn into shallow baking dish and mix the leftover basil and tomato sauce. Spoon the mixture at the top of the loaf and sprinkle cheese over it.Bake

approximately 15 minutes more. Serve warm & enjoy!

Per serving:

Calories: 145

Fat: 9.4g

Saturated Fat: 4.6g

Trans Fat: 4.8g

Carbohydrates: 1g

Fiber: 0.1g

Sodium: 1200mg

Protein: 14.3g

33. Cheese Stuffed Italian Meatloaf

Prepare & ***Cook it in***: *1 hr& 10 mins*

Servings: *8*

Ingredients

- 1 Egg
- 1 Cup Seasoned Dry Bread Crumb
- 1 Teaspoon Minced Garlic
- 1/2 Cup Of Your Favorite Pasta Sauce, Homemade Or In The Jar
- 1 Cup Chopped Onion
- 1/4 Cup Chopped Fresh Basil
- 3/4 Lb Lean Ground Beef
- 1/2 Lb Hot Italian Sausage
- 1 Cup Cubed Mozzarella Cheese, In About 1/4 Inch Pieces
- additional pasta sauce, for garnish

Cooking Instructions

1. Preheat the oven at 350 F/175C.
2. Stir together the 1/2 cup pasta sauce, egg, garlic, and breadcrumbs in a large bowl until all set.
3. Add the leftover ingredients (don't add the ones that are for garnish), and combine with the previous mixture.
4. Transfer the mixture to a large loaf pan andgarnish/top with more pasta sauce. Bake at 175C/350 F approximately an hour.
5. Serve with scalloped potatoes, spaghetti, or rice.

Per serving:

Calories: 145

Fat: 9.4g

Saturated Fat: 4.6g

Trans Fat: 4.8g

Carbohydrates: 1g

Fiber: 0.1g

Sodium: 1200mg

Protein: 14.3g

34. Low-Carb Meatloaf

Prepare & ***Cook it in****: 1 hr& 10 mins*

Servings: *6*

Ingredients

- 1 1/2 Lbs Ground Beef
- 1 Cup Pork Rind, Crumbs
- 1 Egg
- 1/3 Cup Tomato Sauce
- 1/2 Teaspoon Salt
- 1/2 Teaspoon Pepper
- 2 Tablespoons Parsley
- 1/2 Cup Grated Parmesan Cheese
- 1/4 Cup Chopped Onion
- 1/2 Teaspoon Garlic Powder

Cooking Instructions

1. Preheat the oven at 350 F/175C.
2. Mix everything together and shape the mixture into a firm oval loaf in shallow baking pan.
3. Bake approximately an hour and drain off the fat.

Per serving:

Calories: 145

Fat: 9.4g

Saturated Fat: 4.6g

Trans Fat: 4.8g

Carbohydrates: 1g

Fiber: 0.1g

Sodium: 1200mg

Protein: 14.3g

35. Zucchini Meat Loaf

Prepare & ***Cook it in****: 1 hr& 05 mins*

Servings: *6*

Ingredients

FOR THE MEATLOAF

- 2 Eggs, Slightly Beaten
- 2 Cups Zucchini, Shredded
- 1 Cup Plain Breadcrumbs
- 1/3 Cup Onion, Chopped
- 1 Teaspoon Salt

- 1/2 Teaspoon Oregano Leaves, Dried
- 1/4 Teaspoon Pepper
- 1 1/2 Lbs Ground Beef

FOR THE GLAZE

- 1 Tablespoon Brown Sugar, Packed
- 2 Tablespoons Ketchup
- 1/8 Teaspoon Ground Ginger
- 1/8 Teaspoon Cumin

Cooking Instructions

1. Preheat the oven at 350 F/175C.
2. Mix all of the meatloaf ingredients together in a large bowl until well blended and then press the mixture to an deep dish glass pie plate, ungreased (9 1/2 inch).
3. Bake approximately half an hour.
4. In the meantime, mix all of the topping ingredients well in a small bowl.
5. Remove meatloaf from the oven after half an hour &pour the topping over the meatloaf, spread evenly.

6. Put the meatloaf again to oven& bake until a meat thermometer displays 160 F, and thoroughly cooked in center, for 15 more minutes.
7. Before serving, let the meatloaf to stand approximately 5 minutes.

Per serving:

Calories: 145

Fat: 9.4g

Saturated Fat: 4.6g

Trans Fat: 4.8g

Carbohydrates: 1g

Fiber: 0.1g

Sodium: 1200mg

Protein: 14.3g

36. Pizza Style Meatloaf

*Prepare & **Cook it in**: 1 hr& 15 mins*

***Servings:** 8*

Ingredients

- 2 Lbs Lean Ground Beef
- 1 (700 Ml) Jargarden-Style Low-

Carb Pasta Sauce, Divided

- 1/2 Cup Green Pepper, Chopped
- 1/2 Cup Quick-Cooking Oats
- 1 Cup Shredded Part-Skim Mozzarella Cheese, Divided
- 2 Eggs, Lightly Beaten
- Salt And Pepper
- 1/2 Cup Chopped Onion

Cooking Instructions

1. Preheat the oven at 350F/175C. Combine together the 1/2 cup oats, eggs, 1/2 cup cheese, 1/2 cup green peppers, 1 cup sauce, ground beef, pepper and salt in a large bowl.

2. Shape the mixture into a loaf in a baking pan (13 x 9 inch).

3. Top the meatloaf with half cup of sauce.

4. Bake approximately 50 minutes, uncovered.

5. Top with half cup of cheese & then bake for 10 more minutes.

6. Before serving, let the meatloaf to stand approximately 10 minutes.

7. Put the meatloaf to a serving

platter &serve with sauce.

Per serving:

Calories: 145

Fat: 9.4g

Saturated Fat: 4.6g

Trans Fat: 4.8g

Carbohydrates: 1g

Fiber: 0.1g

Sodium: 1200mg

Protein: 14.3g

37. Awesome and Healthy Meatloaf

*Prepare & **Cook it in**: 1 hr*

***Servings:** 4*

Ingredients

- 1 Small Zucchini (Chopped Finely)
- 1/2 Of A Yellow Onion (Chopped Finely)
- 1/2 Of A Red Bell Pepper (Chopped Finely)
- 3 Garlic Cloves (Chopped Finely)
- 1 Teaspoon Salt
- 3 Dashes Pepper

- 1 Teaspoon Dried Thyme
- 1/2 Teaspoon Dried Oregano
- 1/2 Teaspoon Dried Basil
- Cooking Spray
- 1 Lb Lean Ground Beef
- 1 Egg
- 1 Teaspoon Salt
- 1/4 Teaspoon Pepper
- 1 (8 Ounce) Can Tomato Sauce With Basil Garlic And Oregano (Divided)

Cooking Instructions

1. Use cooking spray to spray a skillet.
2. Put zucchini, yellow onion, red bell pepper, garlic cloves, salt, dashes pepper, dried thyme, dried oregano & dried basil in the skillet sauté on medium heat approximately 10 minutes. Let it cool down at room temperature.
3. Mix together the egg, ground beef, pepper, salt, the vegetable mixture and ½ of the tomato sauce in a large bowl.
4. Pat into small meatloaves (approximately seven) &place loafs on a foil lined baking sheet (already sprayed with the cooking spray).
5. Top every loaf with the leftover tomato sauce & bake at 175C/350F approximately half an hour. Serve warm & enjoy!

Per serving:

Calories: 145

Fat: 9.4g

Carbohydrates: 14g

Fiber: 0.1g

Sodium: 1200mg

Protein: 14.3g

38. Maple Sage Meatloaf

*Prepare & **Cook it in**: 1 hr& 30 mins*

***Servings:** 6*

Ingredients

- 1 1/2 lbs ground chuck
- 3/4 cup sour cream
- 1 large egg

- 1/2 cup chopped onion
- 2 tablespoons dried parsley
- 1 teaspoon salt
- 1/2 teaspoon ground sage
- 1/4 cup ketchup (or chili sauce)
- 2 tablespoons maple syrup (or brown sugar)
- 1 teaspoon prepared mustard
- 1 tablespoon barbecue sauce

Cooking Instructions

1. Using your hands, mix together the ground chuck, sour cream, egg, onion, parsley, salt & ground sage until thoroughly mixed (before mixing the chopped onion into the loaf, microwave the onion for approximately 2 minutes on High).
2. In a casserole dish, shape the mixture into a loaf-shape.
3. Combine the leftover ingredients together & then spread at the top of the loaf.
4. Bake at 175C/350F approximately 75 minutes, after 45 minutes, drain off the fat.

Per serving:

Calories: 145

Fat: 9.4g

Saturated Fat: 4.6g

Trans Fat: 4.8g

Carbohydrates: 1g

Fiber: 0.1g

Sodium: 1200mg

Protein: 14.3g

39. Crock Pot Cheesy Meatloaf

*Prepare & **Cook it in**: 8 hrs& 10 mins*

***Servings:** 8*

Ingredients

- 18 Round Cheese Crackers
- 1 Cup Shredded Cheddar Cheese
- 1 Small Onion, Finely Chopped
- 2 Tablespoons Minced Green Peppers
- 1/4 Cup Chili Sauce
- 1/2 Cup Milk
- 2 Eggs, Slightly Beaten
- 3/4 Teaspoon Salt

- 1/8 Teaspoon Pepper
- 2 Lbs Lean Ground Beef

Cooking Instructions

1. Use a blender or rolling pin to crush the crackers.
2. Mix together the chili sauce, shredded cheddar, crushed crackers, green pepper, onion, eggs, milk, pepper, and salt in a large bowl.
3. Add the ground beef & shape the mixture into a round loaf (approximately 7-inch).
4. Place the loaf in a crock pot.
5. Cover; cook on low settings until done, approximately 8 hours.

Calories: 145

Fat: 9.4g

Saturated Fat: 4.6g

Trans Fat: 4.8g

Carbohydrates: 1g

Fiber: 0.1g

Sodium: 1200mg

Protein: 14.3g

40. Easy Stove Top Stuffing Meatloaf

*Prepare & **Cook it in**: 1 hr & 05 mins*

Servings: *6*

Ingredients

- 1 1/2 Lbs Ground Beef
- 1 (6 Ounce) Box Stove Top Stuffing Mix
- 1/2 Cup Water
- 2 Eggs
- 1/3 Cup Ketchup

Cooking Instructions

1. In a large bowl, mix together the ground beef, Stove Top stuffing mix, eggs & water.
2. Pat into a square pan (8x8 inch).
3. Place a very thin layer of ketchup over the top of the loaf.
4. Bake at 175C/350F approximately an hour.

Per serving:

Calories: 145

Fat: 9.4g

Saturated Fat: 4.6g

Trans Fat: 4.8g

Carbohydrates: 1g

Fiber: 0.1g

Sodium: 1200mg

Protein: 14.3g

41. Green olive meatloaf

Prepare & ***Cook it in****: 1 hr& 05 mins*

Servings: *5*

Ingredients

- 1 Lb Ground Turkey
- 1/2 Cup Breadcrumbs
- 1 Egg, Beaten
- 1 Package Onion Soup Mix
- 20 Green Olives, Cut In Half
- 1/2 Cup Ketchup

Cooking Instructions

1. Preheat the oven at 350F/175C.
2. In large bowl, use your hands to mix ground turkey, breadcrumbs, egg, onion soup mix & green olives. Use cooking oil to spray a loaf pan.
3. Shape the mixture into a loaf and put the mixture into a pan.
4. Put the ketchup on &smooth so the loaf is completely covered on the top.
5. Arrange the pan on the middle rack of the oven & bake approximately 50 minutes.

Per serving:

Calories 290

Total fat 23g

Total carbs 0g

Protein 19g

Sodium: 54mg

Potassium 275mg

42. Leftover Meatloaf Parmesan

Prepare & ***Cook it in****: 35 mins*

Servings: *6*

Ingredients

- 4 -6 Slices Leftover Meatloaf
- 1 (15 Ounce) Can Tomato Sauce (Or Your Homemade Stuff)
- 1 Clove Garlic, Minced

- 2 Teaspoons Italian Seasoning
- 4 -6 Slices Mozzarella Cheese

Cooking Instructions

1. Place your meatloaf slices (it may touch but it should not overlap) flat on the bottom of a cooking dish (9x13 inch).
2. Mix together the garlic, tomato sauce, seasoning &pour the mixture at the top of your meatloaf.
3. Over each meatloaf slice, place a slice of cheese.
4. Bake in a 175C/350F oven until the sauce is bubbly and the cheese is browned.

Calories: 145

Fat: 9.4g

Saturated Fat: 4.6g

Trans Fat: 4.8g

Carbohydrates: 1g

Fiber: 0.1g

Sodium: 1200mg

Protein: 14.3g

43. Easy Pork Chops

Prepare it in: 10 minutes

Cook it in: 20 or so minutes

Servings: 4

Ingredients:

- 4 pork chops, boneless
- 1 tablespoon extra-virgin olive oil
- 1 cup chicken stock, low-sodium
- A pinch of black pepper
- 1 teaspoon sweet paprika

INSTRUCTIONS:

1. Heat up a pan while using the oil over medium-high heat, add pork chops, brown them for 5 minutes on either side, add paprika, black pepper and stock, toss, cook for fifteen minutes more, divide between plates and serve by using a side salad.
2. Enjoy!

Per serving:

Calories: 272

Fat: 4

Fiber: 8

Carbs: 14

Protein: 17

44. Coffee BBQ Pork Belly

Prepare it in: 20 minutes

Cook it in: 50 minutes

Servings: 4

Ingredients:

- Beef stock (1.5 cups)
- Low-carb barbecue dry rub (as needed)
- Instant Espresso Powder (2 tbsp.)
- Pork belly (2 lb.)
- Olive oil (4 tbsp.)

Instructions:

1. Set the oven at 350° F.
2. Warm the beef stock in a small saucepan using medium heat until hot - not boiling.
3. Mix in the dry barbecue rub and espresso powder until well combined.
4. Place the pork belly, skin side up in a shallow dish and drizzle half of the oil over the top, rubbing it over the entire pork belly.
5. Pour the hot stock around the pork belly and cover the dish tightly with aluminum foil. Bake it for 45 minutes.
6. Note: Slice into eight thick slices or 16 slices if you like a crispy pork belly.
7. Warm the remaining olive oil in a skillet using med-high heat and sear each slice for three minutes per side or until the desired level of crispiness is reached.

Per serving:

Calories: 644

Protein: 24 g

Fat:

Net Carbohydrates: 3 g

45. Mustard and Rosemary Pork Tenderloin

Prepare it in: 10 minutes

Cook it in: 15 minutes plus 5 minutes resting time

Servings: 4

Ingredients:

- ½ cup fresh parsley leaves
- ¼ cup Dijon mustard
- 6 garlic cloves
- 3 tablespoons fresh rosemary leaves
- 3 tablespoons extra-virgin olive oil
- ½ teaspoon sea salt
- ¼ teaspoon freshly ground black pepper
- 1 (1½-pound) pork tenderloin

Instructions:

1. Preheat the oven to 400°F.
2. In a blender or food processor, combine the parsley, mustard, garlic, rosemary, olive oil, salt, and pepper. Pulse in 1-second pulses, about 20 times, until a paste form. Rub this paste all over the tenderloin and put the pork on a rimmed baking sheet.
3. Bake the pork for about 15 minutes, or until it registers 165°F on an instant-read meat thermometer.
4. Let rest for 5 minutes, slice, and serve.

Per serving:

Calories: 362

Total Fat: 18g

Total Carbs: 5g

Sugar: <1g

Fiber: 2g

Protein: 2g

Sodium: 515mg

46. Stuffed Pork Loin with Sun-Dried Tomato and Goat Cheese

Prepare it in: 15 minutes

Cook it in: 40 minutes

Servings: 6

Ingredients:

- 1 to 1½ pounds pork tenderloin
- 1 cup crumbled goat cheese
- 4 ounces frozen spinach, thawed and well drained
- 2 tablespoons chopped sun-dried tomatoes

- 2 tablespoons extra-virgin olive oil (or seasoned oil marinade from sun-dried tomatoes), plus ¼ cup, divided
- ½ teaspoon salt
- ½ teaspoon freshly ground black pepper
- <u>Zucchini Noodles</u> or sautéed greens, for serving

Instructions:

1. Preheat the oven to 350°F. Cut cooking twine into eight (6-inch) pieces.
2. Cut the pork tenderloin in half lengthwise, leaving about an inch border, being careful to not cut all the way through to the other side. Open the tenderloin like a book to form a large rectangle. Place it between two pieces of parchment paper or plastic wrap and pound to about ¼-inch thickness with a meat mallet, rolling pin, or the back of a heavy spoon.
3. In a small bowl, combine the goat cheese, spinach, sun-dried tomatoes, 2 tablespoons olive oil, salt, and pepper and mix to incorporate well.
4. Spread the filling over the surface of the pork, leaving a 1-inch border from one long edge and both short edges. To roll, start from the long edge with filling and roll towards the opposite edge. Tie cooking twine around the pork to secure it closed, evenly spacing each of the eight pieces of twine along the length of the roll.
5. In a Dutch oven or large oven-safe skillet, heat ¼ cup olive oil over medium-high heat. Add the pork and brown on all sides. Remove from the heat, cover, and bake until the pork is cooked through, 45 to 75 minutes, depending on the thickness of the pork. Remove from the oven and let rest for 10 minutes at room temperature.
6. To serve, remove the twine and

discard. Slice the pork into medallions and serve over Zucchini Noodles or sautéed greens, spooning the cooking oil and any bits of filling that fell out during cooking over top.

Per serving:

Calories: 145

Fat: 9.4g

Saturated Fat: 4.6g

Trans Fat: 4.8g

Carbohydrates: 1g

Fiber: 0.1g

Sodium: 1200mg

Protein: 14.3g

47. Meatballs in Creamy Almond Sauce

Prepare it in: 15 minutes

Cook it in: 35 minutes

Servings: 4-6

Ingredients:

- 8 ounces ground veal or pork
- 8 ounces ground beef
- ½ cup finely minced onion, divided
- 1 large egg, beaten
- ¼ cup almond flour
- 1½ teaspoons salt, divided
- 1 teaspoon garlic powder
- ½ teaspoon freshly ground black pepper
- ½ teaspoon ground nutmeg
- 2 teaspoons chopped fresh flat-leaf Italian parsley, plus ¼ cup, divided
- ½ cup extra-virgin olive oil, divided
- ¼ cup slivered almonds
- 1 cup dry white wine or chicken broth
- ¼ cup unsweetened almond butter

Instructions:

1. In a large bowl, combine the veal, beef, ¼ cup onion, and the egg and mix well with a fork. In a small bowl, whisk together the almond flour, 1 teaspoon salt,

garlic powder, pepper, and nutmeg. Add to the meat mixture along with 2 teaspoons chopped parsley and incorporate well. Form the mixture into small meatballs, about 1 inch in diameter, and place on a plate. Let sit for 10 minutes at room temperature.

2. In a large skillet, heat ¼ cup oil over medium-high heat. Add the meatballs to the hot oil and brown on all sides, cooking in batches if necessary, 2 to 3 minutes per side. Remove from skillet and keep warm.

3. In the hot skillet, sauté the remaining ¼ cup minced onion in the remaining ¼ cup olive oil for 5 minutes. Reduce the heat to medium-low and add the slivered almonds. Sauté until the almonds are golden, another 3 to 5 minutes.

4. In a small bowl, whisk together the white wine, almond butter, and remaining ½ teaspoon salt. Add to the skillet and bring to a boil, stirring constantly. Reduce the heat to low, return the meatballs to skillet, and cover. Cook until the meatballs are cooked through, another 8 to 10 minutes.

5. Remove from the heat, stir in the remaining ¼ cup chopped parsley, and serve the meatballs warm and drizzled with almond sauce.

48. Beef Cacciatore

Prepare it in: 10 minutes

Cook it in: 40 minutes

Servings: 5

Ingredients:

- 1 lb. beef, cut into thin slices
- 1/4 cup extra virgin olive oil
- 1 onion, chopped
- 2 red bell peppers, chopped
- 1 orange bell pepper, chopped
- Salt and pepper, to taste

- 1 cup tomato sauce

Instructions:

1. Place a skillet over a medium heat and add the oil.

2. Add the meat and cook until browned.

3. Add the onions and peppers and cook for 3-5 minutes.

4. Throw in the tomato sauce, salt and pepper, stir well then bring to a simmer.

5. Cover and cook for 40 minutes until the meat is tender.

6. Pour off as much sauce as you can then whizz in a blender.

7. Pour back into the pan and heat again for 5 minutes.

8. Serve with pasta or rice and enjoy.

Calories: 145

Fat: 9.4g

Saturated Fat: 4.6g

Trans Fat: 4.8g

Carbohydrates: 1g

Fiber: 0.1g

Sodium: 1200mg

Protein: 14.3g

49. Meatloaf With Ground Lamb

*Prepare & **Cook it in**: 1hr & 15 mins*

***Servings:** 1*

Ingredients

- 2 Eggs
- 1/2 Cup Dry Breadcrumbs
- 1/2 Teaspoon Salt
- 1/4 Teaspoon Black Pepper
- 1 Lb Ground Beef
- 1 Lb Ground Lamb
- 2 Tablespoons Olive Oil
- 1 Medium Onion, Chopped
- 4 Garlic Cloves, Minced
- 1 Teaspoon Dried Thyme
- 1 Teaspoon Dried Basil
- 1/2 Cup Ketchup Or 1/2 Cup Tomato Paste
- 1 Tablespoon Worcestershire Sauce

Cooking Instructions

1. Preheat your oven at 175C/350F.

2. Sauté the basil, thyme, garlic, and onion in olive oil until the onion are almost golden and soft in a large skillet. Remove the skillet from the heat &let the mixture to cool down slightly.

3. Beat the eggs in a large bowl and add the breadcrumbs, pepper, and salt.

4. Add your cooled garlic, herbs, and onion & the meats, ground.

5. Add the ketchup and Worcestershire sauce.

6. Now, mix together everything &place the mixture in a loaf pan, already greased.

7. Bake approximately an hour.

8. Allow it to cool at room temperature approximately 5 minutes& drain the fat. Serve and enjoy.

Per serving:

Calories 240

Fat 12g

Carbs 7g

Protein 24g

50. Beef & Beans

Prepare it in: 10 minutes

Cook it in: 30 minutes

Servings: 4

Ingredients

- 1 1/2 lbs. beef, cubed
- 8 oz. can tomatoes, chopped
- 8 oz. red beans, soaked overnight, and rinsed
- 1 tsp. garlic, minced
- 1 1/2 cups beef stock
- 1/2 tsp. chili powder
- 1 tbsp. paprika
- 2 tbsp. olive oil, one onion, chopped
- Pepper Salt

Instructions

1. Add oil into the instant pot and set the pot on sauté mode. Add meat and cook for 5 minutes. Add garlic and onion and sauté for 5 minutes.

2. Add remaining ingredients and stir well—seal pot with lid and cook on high for 25 minutes. Once

done, allow to release pressure naturally. Remove lid. Stir well and serve.

Per serving:

Calories 604 Fat 18.7 g

Carbohydrates 41.6 g Sugar 4.5 g

Protein 66.6 g

Cholesterol 152 mg

51. Rosemary Beef Eggplant

Prepare it in: 10 minutes

Cook it in: 30 minutes

Servings: 4

Ingredients

- 1 lb. beef stew meat, cubed
- 2 tbsp. green onion, chopped
- 1/4 tsp. red pepper flakes
- 1/2 tsp. dried rosemary
- 1/2 tsp. paprika
- 1 cup chicken stock
- One onion, chopped
- One eggplant, cubed
- 2 tbsp. olive oil
- Pepper

- Salt

Instructions

1. Add oil into the instant pot and set the pot on sauté mode. Add meat and onion and sauté for 5 minutes. Add remaining ingredients and stir well.

2. Seal pot with lid and cook on high for 25 minutes. Once done, allow to release pressure naturally. Remove lid. Serve and enjoy.

Per serving:

Calories 315 Fat 14.5 g

Carbohydrates 10 g Protein 36.1 g

Cholesterol 101 mg

 Garlic & Thyme Pork Chops

Prepare it in: 10 minutes

Cook it in: 35 minutes

Servings: 4

Ingredients

- 1 tbsp. olive oil
- Four pork loin chops, boneless
- Salt and black pepper to taste
- Four garlic cloves, minced
- 1 tbsp. thyme, chopped

Instructions

1. Preheat the oven to 390 F. Place pork chops, salt, pepper, garlic, thyme, and olive oil in a roasting pan and bake for 10 minutes. Decrease the heat to 360 F and bake for another 25 minutes. Serve with salad.

Per serving:

Calories 170

Fat 6g

Carbs 2g

Protein 26g

52. Sweet & Spicy Pork Chops

Prepare it in: 10 minutes

Cook it in: 20 minutes

Servings: 4

Ingredients

- ½ tsp. cayenne powder
- Four pork chops, boneless
- ¼ cup peach
- 1 tbsp. thyme, chopped
- 2 tbsp. olive oil

Instructions:

1. In a bowl, mix peach preserves, olive oil, and cayenne powder.
2. Preheat your grill to medium heat. Rub pork chops with some peach glaze and grill for 10 minutes. Turn the chops, rub more glazes and cook for another 10 minutes. Serve garnished with thyme.

Per serving:

Calories 240

Fat 12g

Carbs 7g

Protein 24g

53. Pork Loin with Carrots & Snow Peas

Prepare it in: 10 minutes

Cook it in: 20 minutes

Servings: 4

Ingredients

- Two carrots, chopped
- Two garlic cloves, minced
- 1 lb. pork loin, boneless and

cubed

- 4 oz. snow peas
- 2 tbsp. canola oil
- ¾ cup beef stock
- One onion, chopped Salt, and white pepper to taste

Instructions

1. Heat the skillet and put the olive oil over medium heat and sear pork for 5 minutes. Stir in snow peas, carrots, garlic, stock, onion, salt, and pepper and bring to a boil; cook for 15 minutes. Serve right away.

Per serving:

Calories 340 Fat 18g

Carbs 21g

Protein 28g

Chili Lamb Stew

Prepare it in: 10 minutes

Cook it in: 12 minutes

Servings: 4

Ingredients:

- 1 lb. lamb stew, ground Salt, and black pepper to taste
- 2 tbsp. olive oil

- One onion, chopped 2
- garlic cloves, minced
- 1 tbsp. chili paste
- 2 tbsp. balsamic vinegar
- ¼ cup chicken stock
- ¼ cup mint, chopped

Instructions

1. Heat the skillet put the olive oil over medium heat and cook the onion for 3 minutes.

2. Put in lamb stew and cook for another 3 minutes. Stir in salt, pepper, garlic, chili paste, vinegar, stock, and mint and cook for an additional 6 minutes. Serve right away.

Per serving:

Calories 310

Fat 14g

Carbs 16g

Protein 20g

54. Hot Pork Meatballs

Prepare it in: 10 minutes

Cook it in: 20 minutes

Servings: 4

Ingredients:

- 1 lb. ground pork
- 3 tbsp. olive oil
- 2 tbsp. parsley, chopped
- Two green onions, chopped
- Four garlic cloves, minced
- One red chili, chopped
- 1 cup veggie stock
- 2 tbsp. hot paprika

Instructions:

1. Combine pork, parsley, green onions, garlic, and red chili in a bowl and form medium balls out of the mixture.

2. Heat the skillet put the olive oil, set over medium heat. Sear meatballs for 8 minutes on all sides. Stir in stock and hot paprika and simmer for another 12 minutes. Serve warm.

Per serving:

Calories 240

Fat 19g

Carbs 12g

Protein 15g

55. Orange Lamb with Dates

Prepare it in: 30 minutes

Cook it in: 30 minutes

Servings: 4

Ingredients:

- 2 tbsp. olive oil
- 1 tbsp. dates, chopped
- 1 lb. lamb, cubed
- One garlic clove, minced
- One onion, grated
- 2 tbsp. orange juice
- Salt and black pepper to taste
- 1 cup vegetable stock

Instructions:

1. Heat the skillet put the olive oil, set over medium heat and cook onion and garlic for 5 minutes. Put in lamb and cook for another 5 minutes.

2. Stir in dates, orange juice, salt, pepper, and stock and bring to a boil; cook for 20 minutes. Serve right away.

Per serving:

Calories 298 Fat 14g

Carbs 19g

Protein 17g

56. Beef Salad with Green Beans

Prepare it in: 10 minutes

Cook it in: 10 minutes

Servings: 4

Ingredients

- 3/4 pound beef tenderloin, fat trimmed, sliced
- Sea salt to taste
- Ground black pepper, to taste
- 1/2 tsp. red pepper flakes, crushed
- 1 tbsp. olive oil
- 1/2 tsp. dried oregano
- 1/2 tsp. dried rosemary
- 1/2 pound green beans
- One red onion, sliced
- One garlic clove, minced
- 1 Persian cucumber, sliced
- One tomato, sliced
- Two roasted peppers, deseeded and sliced
- One green bell pepper, sliced
- 2 tbsp. fresh parsley, roughly chopped
- 2 tbsp. fresh basil, roughly chopped
- 2 tbsp. fresh mint leaves, roughly chopped
- 1 tbsp. lemon juice
- 4 tbsp. extra-virgin olive oil
- 2 cups butterhead lettuce
- 2 cups baby spinach

Instructions

1. Place the green bean in a saucepan and cover it with cold water (2 inches above them). Bring to a boil and turn the heat to a simmer.

2. Let it simmer for about 5 minutes or until they are crisp-tender; drain the green bean; place them in a bowl of the ice water; drain and reserve.

3. Sprinkle the salt, black pepper, and red pepper evenly over the steaks. Heat the olive oil in a cast-

iron skillet over a high flame.

4. Once hot, cook the stakes for 3 to 4 minutes per side or until browned. Reduce the heat to medium-low; add in the oregano and rosemary and continue to sauté an additional 30 seconds or until fragrant.

5. Cut the steaks into strips and transfer them to a salad bowl. Add in the remaining ingredients and toss to coat.

6. Top with the green beans. Bon appétit!

Per serving:

Calories: 434

Fat: 35.3g

Carbs: 10.5g

Protein: 18.4g

57. Horseradish Meatloaf

*Prepare & **Cook it in**: 1hr & 5 mins*

***Servings:** 8*

Ingredients

FOR MEATLOAF

- 2 Lbs Ground Beef
- 3/4 Cup Regular Oats, Uncooked
- 1 Large Onion, Chopped
- 1/2 Cup Catsup
- 1/4 Cup Milk
- 2 Large Eggs, Lightly Beaten
- 1 Tablespoon Prepared Horseradish
- 1 1/2 Teaspoons Salt
- 1/2 Teaspoon Pepper

FOR SAUCE

- 1/2 cup catsup
- 3 tablespoons brown sugar
- 1 tablespoon prepared horseradish
- 2 teaspoons spicy brown mustard

Cooking Instructions

1. In a large bowl, mix all of the meatloaf ingredients well. Shape the mixture into a loaf& then place in a loaf pan (9x5x3 inch).

2. In a small bowl, mix together all of the sauce ingredients and stir well. Spoon ½ of the sauce mixture at the top of your

meatloaf. Bake at 190C/375 F approximately 50 minutes, uncovered.

3. Spoon the left over mixture of the sauce over the meatloaf bake for 10 more minutes. Remove the meatloaf and put to a serving platter.

Per serving:

Calories 604 Fat 18.7 g

Carbohydrates 41.6 g Sugar 4.5 g

Protein 66.6 g

Cholesterol 152 mg

58. Deer Meatloaf

*Prepare & **Cook it in**: 1hr & 40 mins*

Servings: *6*

Ingredients

- 1 Lb Ground Deer Meat
- 1/2 Lb Lean Sausage Meat
- 3 Slices Soft Bread, Torn Into Pieces
- 1/2 Cup Onion, Chopped
- 1/4 Teaspoon Pepper

- 1/4 Teaspoon Sage
- 1/4 Teaspoon Garlic Salt
- 1 Cup Milk
- 1 1/4 Teaspoons Salt
- 1 Egg
- 1/2 Cup Bell Pepper, Chopped
- 1/4 Teaspoon Dry Mustard
- 1/4 Teaspoon Celery Salt
- 1 Tablespoon Worcestershire Sauce

Cooking Instructions

1. Preheat your oven at 350F/175C.
2. Thoroughly mix all of the ingredients.
3. Bake until done, approximately one and a half hour.

Calories: 145

Fat: 9.4g

Saturated Fat: 4.6g

Trans Fat: 4.8g

Carbohydrates: 1g

Fiber: 0.1g

Sodium: 1200mg

Protein: 14.3g

59. Salsa Meatloaf

*Prepare & **Cook it in**: 50 mins*

***Servings:** 6*

Ingredients

- 1 Lb Lean Ground Beef Or 1 Lb Lean Ground Buffalo
- 1 Egg
- 1 Cup Rolled Oats
- 1 Cup Salsa, From A Jar, Use Your Favorite Kind

Cooking Instructions

1. Thoroughly mix everything and then bake at 175C/350F approximately 45 minutes in an oiled loaf pan.

Per serving:

Calories 457

Fat 19.7 g

Carbohydrates 49.6 g

Sugar 7.5 g

Protein 56.6 g

Cholesterol 152 mg

60. Meatloaf Sandwiches

*Prepare & **Cook it in**: 15 mins*

***Servings:** 1*

Ingredients

- 1/2 Inch Thick Leftover Meatloaf
- 2 Slices Monterey Jack Cheese
- 2 Slices Whole Grain Bread
- Olive Oil

Cooking Instructions

1. Place the slice of your meat loaf between 2 bread slices and2 cheese slices.
2. Use olive oil to brush your sandwich's outside.
3. Cook sandwich over medium low settings in skillet, turning occasionally (4 to 5 minutes each side).

Per serving:

Calories: 434

Fat: 35.3g

Carbs: 10.5g

Protein: 18.4g

61. Afternoon for Two

***Prepare it in**: 10 minutes*

***Cook it in**: 50 minutes*

Servings: 2

Ingredients

- ¼ cup Pancetta-Onion Jam
- 2 tablespoons Cabernet Balsamic Reduction
- 8 ounces burrata (or fresh mozzarella)
- 1 cup arugula
- Sea salt
- Freshly ground black pepper
- Extra-virgin olive oil
- 4 ounces Barolo salami (or any richly seasoned salami), thinly sliced
- 2 small loaves fougasse (or focaccia or ciabatta)
- You will also need: a board, a cheese knife, a small bowl, a small spoon

Instructions

1. Prepare the pancetta-onion jam and cabernet balsamic reduction according to the recipes. The jam can be prepared up to 2 weeks ahead of time, and the reduction up to 3 months ahead of time.

2. Place the burrata in the center of a small board and top with the arugula, letting it naturally cascade around the cheese. Season with salt, pepper, and a drizzle of olive oil. Place the cheese knife next to the burrata.

3. Spoon the pancetta jam in the bottom left corner, near the base of the burrata.

4. Pour the cabernet balsamic reduction into a small bowl and place it in the right top corner with a small spoon in it.

5. Add the salami near the balsamic reduction in the right corner.

6. Cut the bread into small pieces and scatter them in the bottom right corner.

Drink pairing: Cabernet Sauvignon is a scrumptious and fruity full-bodied red wine that is a beautiful complement to the complex flavors of the Barolo salami, pancetta-onion jam, and balsamic reduction. Simply choose your favorite bottle and you cannot go wrong.

62. Beef Noodle Egg Rolls

Prepare it in*: 10 minutes*

Cook it in*: 30 minutes*

Servings: *4*

Ingredients

- 1 pound ground beef
- ½ cup dry Chow Mein noodles
- 2 celery stalks, finely chopped
- 3 cloves garlic, minced
- 2 tablespoons fresh ginger, grated
- 1 cup cabbage, shredded
- 2 green onions, chopped
- 3 tablespoons soy sauce
- 1 tablespoon Hoisin sauce
- 1 teaspoon black pepper
- Extra light olive oil
- 12 egg roll wrappers

Instructions

1. Soak Chow Mein in warm water.
2. Heat oil in a skillet over medium heat.
3. Add garlic and onion, and stir-fry for 30 seconds to a minute until tender and fragrant. Add ground beef, brown, and remove from heat.
4. Add cabbage, Chow Mein noodles, and ginger to the skillet along with hoisin sauce, pepper, and soy sauce.
5. Place one heaping tablespoon of filling about three inches above the bottom corner, roll the bottom corner over the wrapper and fold over the left side and then the right side over the wrapper, continue to roll up to one inch below the top corner, brush the top edges with water and flour mixture and seal wrapper, repeat.
6. Fill a heavy frying pot halfway with oil, or you can also fry the egg rolls in a wok. Let the oil reach 350ºF. Deep fry egg rolls until golden brown, about 1-2

minutes per side. You can also use a deep-frying machine.

7. Serve with your favorite dipping sauce.

Per serving:

Calories: 434

Fat: 35.3g

Carbs: 10.5g

Protein: 18.4g

63. South of France

Prepare it in: *10 minutes*

Cook it in: *20 minutes*

Servings: *3*

Ingredients

- 12 ounces Duck Confit
- ½ cup Mustard Gastrique
- 8 ounces Fromage blanc (or quark)
- 2 ounces caviar
- 4 large hard-boiled eggs, diced small
- 1 small red onion, minced
- 6 ounces black pepper crackers
- You will also need: a large platter,

2 small bowls, a small serving fork, 2 small spoons, a small dish, a caviar spoon, 4 small teaspoons

Instructions

1. Prepare the duck confit and mustard gastrique according to the recipes. The confit can be prepared up to 3 months ahead of time and reheated, and the gastrique can be prepared up to 2 weeks ahead of time and reheated.

2. Put the warm duck confit in a small bowl with a serving fork, and place the bowl on the top left side of the board.

3. Place the Fromage blanc in a small bowl with a spoon on the bottom right side of the board.

4. Place the caviar in a small bowl in the center of the board, with the caviar spoon in it. Place the teaspoons beside it.

5. To the left of the caviar, place the diced hard-boiled eggs. Just above the eggs, place the minced

red onion.

6. Below the caviar, spoon the warm mustard gastrique directly onto the board, then use the back of the spoon to pull it to the right, creating an artful look. Leave the spoon to the side.

7. Arrange the crackers in both the upper right and lower left quadrants.

Drink pairing: A delicate and fruity champagne will provide a crisp, refreshing contrast to the flavors of this board. We recommend Le Mesnil Blanc de Blancs Grand Cru, which has a subtle fruitiness perfumed with hints of apple and pear and is readily available online.

Ingredient tip: You can use whatever kind of caviar appeals to you. Unopened caviar can be stored in the refrigerator for about 2 weeks.

Calories: 145

Fat: 9.4g

Saturated Fat: 4.6g

Trans Fat: 4.8g

Carbohydrates: 1g

Fiber: 0.1g

Sodium: 1200mg

Protein: 14.3g

64. The Sicilian Table

Prepare it in*: 10 minutes*

Cook it in*: 40 minutes*

Servings: *6*

Ingredients

- 2 cups Rosemary-Lemon Castelvetrano Olives
- 1 Artisan Focaccia, cut into large squares
- 1 (4-ounce) log goat cheese
- ¼ cup chopped salted pistachios
- 5½ ounces salami with pistachios (or any flavorful salami), sliced
- 5½ ounces fennel salami (or any herb-infused salami), sliced
- You will also need: a large board, a small cheese knife, a medium bowl, a spoon

Instructions

1. Prepare the rosemary-lemon olives and artisan focaccia according to the recipes. The olives can be prepared up to a week ahead of time, but the focaccia is best served warm or at room temperature.

2. Roll the log of goat cheese in the chopped pistachios. Place the log to the left-center of the board. Stick a small cheese knife on the top of it.

3. Place the pistachio salami slices in the left bottom corner of the board.

4. Place the fennel salami in the bottom right corner of the board.

5. Fill a medium bowl with the marinated olives, add a spoon, and place it in the top right area of the board.

6. Scatter the focaccia squares along the top of the board, reaching from side to side.

Drink pairing: Keeping with the theme, you can pair this board with some olive vermouth, the sister to the well-known dirty martini. It's a briny cocktail that will complement the citrus notes of the olives and the saltiness of the salami. In a tumbler, combine ⅔ ounce dry vermouth, ⅓ ounce fresh orange juice, 1 ounce of scotch whiskey, and a few ice cubes. Stir well for about 20 seconds. Strain into a cocktail glass and finish with 3 Castelvetrano olives on a stick. A mocktail version can be made with white grape juice in place of the vermouth and a splash of cream soda in place of the scotch.

Per serving:

Calories 457

Fat 19.7 g

Carbohydrates 49.6 g

Sugar 7.5 g

Protein 56.6 g

Cholesterol 152 mg

65. Happy Hour Tapas

Prepare it in: 10 minutes

Cook it in: 50 minutes

Servings: 4

Ingredients

For the chili oil Manchego

12 ounces Manchego (or any mild sheep milk cheese), cut into bite-size pieces

- 1 fresh chile, thinly sliced
- 1 cup extra-virgin olive oil
  For the crushed tomato crostini
- 1 baguette, sliced
- 1 garlic clove, cut in half
- Extra-virgin olive oil, for drizzling
- 1 large, ripe heirloom tomato

For the board

- ½ Spanish Tortilla
- 1 cup arugula
- Extra-virgin olive oil, for drizzling
- Freshly ground black pepper
- Sea salt
- 6 ounces salchichón ibérico (or any Spanish hard salami), sliced
- 6 ounces chorizo, sliced
- You will also need: a medium board, a jar with a cover, a small fork

Instructions

To make the chili oil Manchego:

1. Put the Manchego pieces in a medium jar. Add the chile slices and pour in the olive oil, making sure the cheese is submerged.

2. Screw on the lid and set aside for at least 1 hour so the oil and peppers can infuse fully into the cheese.

To make the crushed tomato crostini:

1. Preheat the oven to 375°F.

2. Spread out the baguette slices on a rimmed baking sheet. Toast in the oven for 7 minutes.

3. Rub one side of each slice with a cut garlic clove and drizzle with olive oil.

4. In a food processor or blender, pulse the tomato until it resembles a coarse salsa.

To make the board:

1. Prepare the Spanish tortilla according to the recipe. The tortilla can be prepared the day before and reheated. Cut it into 1-by-2-inch rectangles and place the pieces in the center of the board. Top with the arugula, a drizzle of olive oil, and a few grinds of black pepper.

2. Place the crostini along the bottom of the board, from the center to the right side. Spoon the tomato puree over the crostini and season with sea salt and freshly ground black pepper.

3. Place the salchichón ibérico slices in the top right area of the board.

4. Place the chorizo slices in the bottom left corner of the board. Put a small fork in the jar of Manchego and place it in the top left.

   Drink pairing: A young or aged Tempranillo, a full-bodied Spanish red wine, would be a great choice for this board. Depending on your preference, you could also go with a young, fruitier version or an aged, bold, high-tannin wine with hints of cherry, fig, and cedar.

Per serving:

Calories 457

Fat 19.7 g

Carbohydrates 49.6 g

Sugar 7.5 g

Protein 56.6 g

Cholesterol 152 mg

66. Ground Beef Canapés

Prepare it in: *10 minutes*

Cook it in: *60 minutes*

Servings: *4*

Ingredients

- 3 tablespoons olive oil
- 1 pound of lean ground beef
- Salt and pepper to taste
- 1 teaspoon dried thyme
- 1 teaspoon dried basil

- 1 tablespoon BBQ sauce
- 1 teaspoon Dijon mustard
- 1 cup tomato sauce
- 3 tablespoons freshly chopped parsley
- 7 ounces crackers

Instructions

1. Using a nonstick pan heat the butter
2. Add the ground beef and cook it for about 10 minutes.
3. Season with salt and pepper, thyme, basil, BBQ sauce, Dijon mustard, and tomato sauce.
4. Cook for 5 minutes and sprinkle in the parsley.
5. Let cool completely and serve on.

   Per serving: Calories 357, Fat 23.7, Fiber 3.3, Carbs 11.4, Protein 26.3

67. Sour Then Sweet

Prepare it in: *10 minutes*
Cook it in: *30 minutes*
Servings: *3*

Ingredients

- 4 cups Brined Cucumber Ribbons
- 2 cups Spiced Candied Nuts
- 8 ounces SeaHive cheddar (or any mild white cheddar)
- 8 ounces pickled herring
- 8 ounces mascarpone
- ¼ cup honey
- 2 Granny Smith apples, cored and sliced
- 1 sourdough baguette
- You will also need: a large board, a small cheese knife, a pint-size canning jar, 2 small cocktail forks, a small dish, a small bowl, a small spreading knife or spoon, a small honey jar, a honey wand

Instructions

1. Prepare the brined cucumber ribbons and spiced candied nuts according to the recipes. The cucumbers can be prepared up to a week ahead of time and the nuts up to 3 months.
2. Place the cheddar in the bottom right corner of the board with a

small cheese knife next to it.

3. Place the brined cucumber ribbons in a pint-size jar below the top left corner. Add a small cocktail fork to the jar.

4. Put the pickled herring into a small dish with a cocktail fork, and place it next to the cucumber ribbons but slightly offset.

5. In the top center of the board, place the mascarpone in a bowl with a small spreading knife or spoon.

6. Put the honey in a small jar with a honey wand, and place it to the right of the mascarpone.

7. Sprinkle the candied nuts near the cheddar in the bottom center of the board.

8. Place the Granny Smith slices in the center of the board.

9. Tear the baguette into large pieces and place them along the top right side of the board near the herring.

Drink pairing: A green appletini is the perfect sour and sweet drink to accompany this arrangement. In a cocktail shaker, combine 1 ounce Smirnoff Green Apple Vodka, ½ ounce sour mix, 3 ounces apple cider, and some ice cubes. Shake well, then strain into a cocktail glass and coat the rim with a 1-to-2 salt-to-sugar ratio. Garnish with a small wedge of Granny Smith apple.

Per serving:

Calories 457

Fat 19.7 g

Carbohydrates 49.6 g

Sugar 7.5 g

Protein 56.6 g

Cholesterol 152 mg

Lunch and Dinner Recipes

68. Mushrooms and Beef Egg Roll

Prepare it in: *10 minutes*

Cook it in: *30 minutes*

Servings: 10

Ingredients

- 1 onion, diced
- 1 tablespoon olive oil
- 2 baby Bella mushrooms, chopped
- ½ pound ground beef
- 4 teaspoons soya sauce
- 1 cup green cabbage, shredded
- 1 teaspoon chili garlic sauce
- 2 teaspoons ground black pepper, fresh
- 10 egg roll wrappers defrosted
- 1 teaspoon sesame oil
- 1 tablespoon water, 1 egg, beaten together
- Oil for frying

Instructions

1. In a frying pan or a wok, warm the olive oil on medium heat. Add the beef.
2. Cook the beef till it browns, around 8-10 minutes.
3. Add onions, mushrooms, and cabbage to the pan. Stir-fry for another 5 minutes.
4. Remove the pan from the heat, and add soya sauce, chili garlic sauce, and sesame oil.
5. Take an egg roll wrap and place it on a dry and flat surface.
6. Place around 2-3 tablespoons of the mixture in the middle of the wrap.
7. Roll the wrap tightly and seal the ends using the egg and water mixture.
8. Do the same for all the wraps.
9. Once the oil has heated to 350ºF177ºC, fry the egg rolls in batches. Do not overcrowd the saucepan.
10. Fry on all sides till golden and crisp.

Per serving:

Calories: 469

Fat: 23.1g

Saturated Fat: 5.8g

Trans Fat: 17.3g

Carbohydrates: 0.9g

Fiber: 0.2g

Sodium: 210mg

Protein: 60.7g

69. Beef and Caramelized Scallion Fried Dumplings

Prepare it in: 10 minutes

Cook it in: 30 minutes

Servings: 4

Ingredients

- ¾ pound ground beef
- 1 cup beans sprouts, roughly chopped
- 3 green onions, finely chopped
- 1 tablespoon ginger, grated
- 4 tablespoons low-sodium soy sauce
- 1 teaspoon black pepper
- 1 egg, beaten
- Extra light olive oil
- 14 dumpling wrappers

Instructions

1. Heat the oil over medium heat, add scallions, sauté for 30 seconds.

2. Sprinkle scallions with brown sugar, and give a quick sauté.

3. Add ground beef and brown.

4. Add ginger, scallions, sauté for a minute.

5. Add soy sauce, black pepper, mung bean sprouts, and green cabbage, mix and remove from heat.

6. Bring the bottom half up over the filling to meet the top half and pinch the two halves together in the center, then pinch together the sides.

7. Place dumplings on a plate and cover them with a slightly damp cloth to ensure they do not dry out.

8. Fill a large pot of water up

halfway over medium heat and bring to a boil.

9. Drop a batch of dumplings into the water and cook for 10 minutes. Leave raw dumplings under a damp cloth.

10. Serve warm with a dipping sauce like the spicy peanut sauce.

Per serving:

Calories 457

Fat 19.7 g

Carbohydrates 49.6 g

Sugar 7.5 g

Protein 56.6 g

Cholesterol 152 mg

70. Cheese and Beef Chips

Prepare it in: *10 minutes*

Cook it in: *30 minutes*

Servings: *4*

Ingredients

- ½ pound lean ground beef
- Salt and pepper to taste
- 1½ cups shredded cheddar

cheese

- 1 teaspoon dried oregano
- 1 teaspoon dried basil
- ½ teaspoon garlic powder
- 1 teaspoon chili flakes
- 1 teaspoon paprika
- 3 tablespoons olive oil

Instructions

1. Add the ground meat, salt, and pepper, cheese, oregano, basil, garlic powder, chili flakes, and paprika to a large bowl.

2. Mix until everything is combined.

3. Grease a 15-inch casserole pan or skillet with olive oil and spread the mixture evenly into it with an offset spatula.

4. Let cool slightly and cut as desired

71. Grilled Whole Chicken

Prep Time: 15 mins

Cook it in: 1 hour 20 minutes

Servings: 6

Ingredients:

1 (4-pound) whole chicken, neck and giblets removed

3 tablespoons butter, melted

Salt and freshly ground black pepper, to taste

Instructions:

1. Preheat the grill for indirect heat. Adjust the temperature to 350-400 degrees in the indirect area.

2. Grease the grill grate.

3. Coat the chicken with about 1½ tablespoons of butter and then season with salt and black pepper.

4. Arrange the chicken over the indirect heat, angling one thigh and leg to the direct heat side.

5. Close the grill with lid and cook for about 40 minutes.

6. Rotate the bird, angling the other thigh towards the heat and coat with the remaining butter.

7. Cook for about 40 minutes more.

8. Remove from the grill and place the chicken onto a cutting board for about 5-10 minutes before carving.

9. With a sharp knife, cut the chicken into desired-sized pieces and serve.

Per serving:

Calories: 508

Fat: 14.9g

Saturated Fat: 6.2g

Trans Fat: 8.7g

Carbohydrates: 0g

Fiber: 0g

Sodium: 259mg

Protein: 87.7g

72. Beef Patty Lettuce Wraps

Prepare it in: *10 minutes*

Cook it in: *60 minutes*

Servings: *4*

Ingredients

- 8 Bibb lettuce leaves
- ½ avocado
- 1 pound 90% lean ground beef
- ¼ teaspoon pepper

- ½ teaspoon salt
- ⅓ cup feta cheese, crumbled
- 2 tablespoons low-carb mayonnaise
- ¼ cup chopped red onion
- Chopped cherry tomatoes (optional)
- ½ avocados

Instructions

1. Add the beef in, salt, and pepper to a mixing bowl; mix well.
2. Prepare 8 patties from the mixture.
3. Preheat the grill to medium-high heat.
4. Grill the patties for 4 minutes on each side until evenly brown.
5. Arrange the lettuce leaves and place the patties over them.
6. In a bowl, combine the mayonnaise and feta cheese. Spread over the patties.
7. Top with red onion, avocado, and optionally with tomatoes. Serve fresh.

Per serving: Calories 357, Fat 23.7, Fiber 3.3, Carbs 11.4, Protein 26.3

73. Hiyashi Chuka Cold Ramen

Prepare it in: *10 minutes*

Cook it in: *40 minutes*

Servings: *3*

Ingredients

For the ramen:

- 2 portions ramen noodles
- 1/2 cucumber, thinly sliced
- 4 sticks crab meat, shredded into thin strips
- 1/4 lb. shrimp, shelled and deveined
- 1/2 tomato, sliced
- 50 g ham, cut into strips
- 2 eggs

For the sesame dressing:

- 1 teaspoon Chicken Gara soup stock powder
- 100 ml hot water
- 4 tablespoon white sesame seeds paste

- 2 tablespoons soy sauce
- 3 tablespoons sugar
- 3 tablespoons rice wine vinegar
- 2 teaspoons sesame oil
- 2 teaspoons sesame seeds

For the soy sauce vinaigrette:

- 1 teaspoon Chicken Gara soup stock powder
- 1/3 cup ml hot water
- 6 tablespoon soy sauce
- 3 tablespoons vinegar
- 3 tablespoons sugar
- 2 tablespoons sesame seed oil

For the garnish:

- 2 tablespoons pickled ginger
- 1 tablespoon chopped scallions
- 1 tablespoon Japanese kewpie mayonnaise
- 1/2 teaspoon mustard
- 1 teaspoon white sesame seeds

Instructions

1. Mix chicken Gara powder and hot water until fully dissolved in a bowl.
2. Add remaining ingredients for soy sauce vinaigrette and mix.

Chill in the fridge.

3. Fry eggs in a thin layer and cut them into thin strips. Set it aside to cool down.
4. Cook noodles per instructions and let cool.
5. Assemble by placing chilled noodles in a bowl, then top with shrimp, crab meat, egg, cucumber, tomato, and ham.
6. Garnish with ginger, lemon slice, and scallion. Pour sesame dressing over the top and sprinkle with sesame seeds.
7. Serve with Japanese mayonnaise and mustard.

Per serving:

Calories: 469

Fat: 23.1g

Saturated Fat: 5.8g

Trans Fat: 17.3g

Carbohydrates: 0.9g

Fiber: 0.2g

Sodium: 210mg

Protein: 60.7g

74. Okinawa Soba

Prepare it in: 10 minutes

Cook it in: 40 minutes

Servings: 3

Ingredients

For the broth:

- 14 oz. pork belly block
- 4 cups water for pre-boiling
- 6 cups water for the broth

For the Katsuo Dashi:

- 2 cups water
- 1 cup katsuobushi
- For the soup broth:
- 1/2 tablespoon sea salt
- 2 teaspoons soy sauce
- For the stewed pork belly:
- 2 tablespoons black sugar
- 2 tablespoons awamori
- 2 tablespoons soy sauce
- 2 tablespoons water

For the Okinawa Soba:

- 2 servings noodles
- green onion/scallion, chopped, to taste
- sliced fish cakes, to taste

Instructions

1. Put pork belly in a large pot and add enough water to cover the meat. Bring the water to a boil.

2. Once boiling, switch heat to low and simmer for 3-5 minutes, until it foams and scum floats on the surface. Drain and rinse the pork and the pot under running water.

3. Return meat to the same pot, and add 6 cups of water. Bring it to a boil.

4. When it's boiling, simmer for 1 hour, skimming off scum and foam from the surface.

5. At the same time, bring 2 cups of water to a boil in a small saucepan. Turn heat to low, add katsuobushi, and let simmer for 15 seconds. Turn off heat. Set aside to steep until ready to use.

6. Remove pork from the pot and cover it with foil. Set aside to cool.

7. Strain the broth through a fine sieve. Put 4 cups of pork broth

back in the pot.

8. Strain bonito flakes water through the sieve. Bring the broth to a boil.

9. Once boiling, switch to low heat and add 2 teaspoons soy sauce and 1 tablespoon salt. Mix well and adjust salt if needed. Turn off and cover the pot with a lid. Set aside.

10. When pork belly is cool enough, cut into thin 1-inch slices.

11. Add 2 tablespoons of black sugar, 2 tablespoons of awamori, 2 tablespoons soy sauce, and 2 tablespoons of water. Mix well and bring to a boil. Lower heat and add pork slices, quickly coating with sauce.

12. Cover with lid and cook for 25-30 minutes on low, until sauce has almost evaporated.

13. Cook noodles according to the package Instructions. Drain the noodles.

14. Place the noodles in a bowl. Pour soup broth over the noodles and top with pork belly slices, green onions, and fish cake.

Per serving:

Calories 457

Fat 19.7 g

Carbohydrates 49.6 g

Sugar 7.5 g

Protein 56.6 g

Cholesterol 152 mg

75. Homemade Tonkotsu Ramen

***Prepare it in**: 10 minutes*

***Cook it in**: 40 minutes*

***Servings:** 3*

Ingredients

For the broth:

- 6 lbs. pork bones
- 1 onion, peeled and halved

For the miso tare:

- 1/2 cup Shiro miso
- 1/4 cup sake
- 1/4 cup mirin
- 1 teaspoon kosher salt

For the ramen:

- 8 cups homemade pork broth
- 12 oz. dried ramen noodles
- 4 large hard-boiled eggs
- 12 Cha Shu pork slices
- 2 oz. dried shiitake mushrooms
- 1/2 cup bamboo shoots
- 1 green onion, sliced
- 4 nori sheets

Instructions

1. Cover pork bones with cold water in a large stockpot. Bring to a boil over medium heat, then discard water and rinse bones in cold water. Return bones to the stockpot, cover with water and bring to a boil. Then lower heat to medium.

2. Add onion, and cover the pot. Cook for 10-12 hours over medium heat, adding water as needed to keep the bones covered.

3. Remove bones, strain the broth, and let it cool to room temperature.

4. Add miso, sake, mirin, and salt into a small saucepan. Bring to a simmer and cook for 5 minutes. Set aside.

5. Cook noodles, following Instructions on the package.

6. Rehydrate mushrooms in boiling water and set them aside.

7. Heat a large skillet and brown sliced pork on all sides.

8. Divide the miso tare into four bowls. Top with 1/2 cup broth and mix well.

9. Add noodles and 1 1/2 cups broth.

10. Top with egg, nori, mushrooms, pork, and green onions.

11. Can be stored for 4 months in the freezer.

Per serving:

Calories: 469

Fat: 23.1g

Saturated Fat: 5.8g

Trans Fat: 17.3g

Carbohydrates: 0.9g

Fiber: 0.2g

Sodium: 210mg   Protein: 60.7g

Protein Recipes (Fish & Meat)

76. Seafood Bake

Prep Time: 15 mins

Cook it in: 30 mins

Servings: 6

Ingredients:

12 ounces imitation lobster meat

12 ounces imitation crab meat

6 ounces shrimp, peeled and deveined

1 cup mayonnaise

2 tablespoons scallions, sliced

½ cup Mozzarella cheese, shredded

Instructions:

1. Preheat the oven to 350 degrees F. Grease a baking dish.
2. In a large bowl, add the seafood, mayonnaise and scallion and stir to combine.
3. Place the seafood mixture into the prepared baking dish evenly and top with Mozzarella cheese.
4. Bake for approximately 25-30 minutes.
5. Serve hot.

Per serving:

Calories: 382

Fat: 29.1g

Saturated Fat: 4.5g

Trans Fat: 24.6g

Carbohydrates: 1.7g

Fiber: 0.1g

Sodium: 954mg

Protein: 25g

77. Baked Trout

Prep Time: 15 mins

Cook it in: 25 mins

Servings: 6

Ingredients:

2 (1½-pound) wild-caught trout, gutted and cleaned

Salt and freshly ground black pepper, to taste

1 lemon, sliced

2 tablespoons fresh dill, minced

2 tablespoons butter, melted

2 tablespoons fresh lemon juice

Instructions:

1. Preheat the oven to 475 degrees F. Arrange a wire rack onto a foil-lined baking sheet.
2. Sprinkle the trout with salt and black pepper from inside and outside generously.
1. Fill the cavity of each fish with lemon slices and dill.
2. Place the trout onto the prepared baking sheet and drizzle with the melted butter and lemon juice.
3. Bake for about 25 minutes.
4. Remove the baking sheet from oven and transfer the trout onto a serving platter.
5. Serve hot.

Per serving:

Calories: 469

Fat: 23.1g

Saturated Fat: 5.8g

Trans Fat: 17.3g

Carbohydrates: 0.9g

Fiber: 0.2g

Sodium: 210mg

Protein: 60.7g

78. Tonkotsu Miso Ramen

***Prepare it in**: 10 minutes*

***Cook it in**: 40 minutes*

***Servings:** 3*

Ingredients

For the broth:

- 2 1/2 cups Tonkotsu base
- 2 tablespoons white miso
- 1 tablespoon tahini
- 2 teaspoons sesame oil
- 2 cloves garlic, grated
- 1/2 cup water
- 2 tablespoons pork fat, minced

For the toppings:

- 1 tablespoon ground sesame seeds
- 1/2 ramen noodles
- 12 Cha Shu pork slices
- garlic chives
- 1 bunch scallions, chopped
- 1/4 cup sweet corn
- 2 oz. dried shiitake mushrooms,

rehydrated and sliced

- 1 ramen egg
- 2 large dried scallops

Instructions

1. Heat Tonkotsu Base in a medium saucepan.

2. Mix miso, sesame oil, tahini, and garlic in a small bowl, whisk in water. Pour the mixture into a hot Tonkotsu Base and whisk well. Once it's creamy and smooth without any chunks, add pork fat and whisk. Adjust salt to taste. If it's too concentrated, thin it out with water.

3. Divide cooked noodles between two bowls. Add ground sesame seeds to the soup and whisk one more time, then pour over noodles.

4. Top with listed or toppings and grate dried scallop over each bowl before serving.

Per serving:

Calories 457

Fat 19.7 g

Carbohydrates 49.6 g

Sugar 7.5 g

Protein 56.6 g

Cholesterol 152 mg

79. Creamy Tonkotsu Ramen

Prepare it in: *10 minutes*

Cook it in: *40 minutes*

Servings: *3*

Ingredients

- 1 large onion, skin on, chopped
- 1 3-inch knob ginger, chopped
- 2 whole leeks, washed and chopped
- 2 dozen scallions, chopped
- 6 halved ramen eggs
- 2 tablespoons vegetable oil
- 12 garlic cloves
- 6 oz. enoki mushrooms
- 1 lb. slab pork fatback
- 2 lbs. chicken carcasses and backs, skin and fat removed
- 3 lbs. pig trotters, cut crosswise into 1-inch disks

Instructions

1. Heat oil in a nonstick skillet over high heat. Add garlic, onions, and ginger. Cook for 15 minutes, tossing occasionally. Set aside.

2. Add chicken and pork bones to a large stockpot and cover with cold water. Bring to a boil over high heat, then remove from heat and discard water.

3. Wash all bones under cold water, removing coagulated blood or any bits of dark marrow. Bones should become uniform grey or white after scrubbing.

4. Return bones to pot with pork fatback, scallion whites, charred vegetables, leeks, and mushrooms. Cover with cold water. Bring to a rolling boil over high heat, skimming off any scum. Wipe any scum off from around the rim of the pot with a paper towel. Switch heat to low, let simmer and place a heavy lid on top.

5. Check the broth after 15 minutes. If it's not a slow rolling boil, increase or decrease the heat to adjust the boiling speed. Boil for 4 hours, until fatback is fully tender.

6. Remove pork fat with a slotted spatula and place it in a sealed container in the fridge.

7. Cover the pot and cook for 6-8 hours, until broth is opaque with the texture of light cream, adding more water to keep bones covered.

8. When broth is ready, turn to high heat and cook until reduced to 3 quarts. Strain into a clean pot. Repeat if you want cleaner broth. Discard any solids and fat with a ladle. Roughly chop pork fatback and whisk into broth.

9. To serve, season soup with condiments of choice and serve with cooked ramen noodles and preferable toppings.

Per serving:

Calories: 382

Fat: 29.1g

Saturated Fat: 4.5g

Trans Fat: 24.6g

Carbohydrates: 1.7g

Fiber: 0.1g

Sodium: 954mg

Protein: 25g

80. Tonkotsu Toridashi Ramen

Prepare it in: *10 minutes*

Cook it in: *40 minutes*

Servings: *3*

Ingredients

- 10 oz. ramen noodles
- 2 tablespoon sesame oil
- 10 shiitake mushrooms, cut into slithers
- 4 1/2 pints toridashi stock
- 1oz. ginger, cut into 4 slices
- 3 ½ oz. shimeji mushrooms
- 1 carrot, cut into matchsticks
- 7 oz. soya bean sprouts
- 1 1/2 bamboo shoots, sliced

- 2 garlic cloves, sliced
- 3 ½ oz. enoki mushrooms
- 16 slices Cha Shu pork
- 4 spring onion, cut on the diagonal
- 7 oz. Choi Sum, trimmed and cut in half
- 1 red chili, finely sliced on a diagonal
- 4 whole tomago eggs, halved
  For the serving:
- Japanese chili oil
- shichimi togarashi (Japanese seven-spice seasoning)
- dried tuna flakes
  For the Toridashi stock:
- 3lb 5oz. chicken wings
- 3lb 5oz. pork bones
- 10g piece dried kombu
- 2 thick slices of fresh root ginger
- 9 oz. of sake
- 1 medium onion, cut in half
- 1oz. bonito flakes (katsuobushi)
- 6 dried shiitake mushrooms

Instructions

1. Preheat the oven to 375°F.

2. Arrange pork bones and chicken wings in a roasting pan and roast for 30-40 minutes, turning them halfway through, until golden brown.

3. Place wings and bones in a large sieve, then pour boiling water over bones to remove excess grease.

4. While chicken is in the oven, rinse kombu under cold water. Soak kombu in a large pot for 30 minutes in 4 1/2 pints cold water.

5. Remove kombu from water and cut into three long strips. Return to the stockpot and bring to a simmer. Remove from heat and discard kombu.

6. Add wings, bones, and all remaining ingredients to kombu water. Bring it to a boil, cover with a lid and simmer for 2 hours on low.

7. Strain the stock through a fine-mesh strainer. Leave for 10 minutes to drain, cool, and set in the fridge until you need it.

8. Cook noodles following the Instructions on the packet. Drain and drizzle with sesame oil.

9. Heat stock in a pan with ginger, garlic, mushrooms, and carrots. Simmer for 5-8 minutes. Add shimeji mushrooms.

10. Place noodles, bamboo shoots, beansprouts, enoki mushrooms, Choi Sum, and sliced pork in serving bowls. Ladle stock over the noodles. Sprinkle with spring onions, shichimi togarashi, and sliced chili. Top with halved tamago egg and serve.

Per serving:

Calories: 434

Fat: 35.3g

Carbs: 10.5g

Protein: 18.4g

81. Tonkotsu Shio Ramen

Prepare it in: *10 minutes*

Cook it in: *40 minutes*

Servings: *3*

Ingredients

- 10 oz. ramen noodles
- 4 lbs. pork feet, cut to expose the bone marrow
- 6 ramen eggs
- 12 Cha Shu pork slices
- 1 cup sweet corn
- 1 bunch chopped green onion
  For the Shio tare:
- 2 tablespoons sea salt
- 2 tablespoons sake
- 1 tablespoon mirin
- 2 teaspoons sesame oil
- 1 teaspoon soy sauce
- 1 garlic clove, crushed

Instructions

1. Place pork feet in a big pot and cover with water (1-2 inches above the bones). Boil for 15 min, stirring. Remove all the junk from the surface.

2. Remove from heat and strain the bones. Clean coagulated blood or dark marrow with the end of a chopstick or toothbrush.

3. Return bones to the pot and cover with water a few inches above them. Bring to a rolling boil, lower the heat and simmer for 16 hours.

4. Mix all tare ingredients and add a spoonful to the bottom of each serving bowl. Add the broth and season with more tare if needed.

5. Boil noodles according to the Instructions on a package and drain them.

6. Divide noodles between bowls, top with sliced pork, ramen egg, sweet corn, and chopped green onion.

Per serving:

Calories 457

Fat 19.7 g

Carbohydrates 49.6 g

Sugar 7.5 g

Protein 56.6 g

Cholesterol 152 mg

82. Yummy Pork Noodle Casserole

Prepare it in*: 10 minutes*

Cook it in*: 40 minutes*

Servings: *3*

Ingredients

- 2 cups egg noodles
- cooking spray
- 3 tablespoons butter
- 1/4 cup chopped onion
- 1/4 cup chopped celery
- 1/4 cup chopped carrots
- 1/4 cup chopped red bell pepper
- 2 (10.75 ounces) cans condensed cream of chicken soup
- 1/2 cup sour cream, or more to taste
- 2 cups shredded Cheddar cheese
- 1 (8 ounces) can whole kernel corn, drained
- 3 cups cubed cooked pork
- 1 teaspoon salt
- 1/4 teaspoon ground black pepper
- 1/2 cup dry bread crumbs (optional)

Direction

1. Bring lightly salted water in a big pot over high heat to a rolling boil. When water is boiling, mix in egg noodles, and bring back to a boil. Cook pasta without a cover for 5 minutes, mixing from time to time, till noodles have cooked through, yet are firm to the bite. Drain thoroughly in a colander placed in the sink.

2. Preheat the oven to 175 °C or 350 °F. With cooking spray, coat a 9x13-inch baking pan.

3. In a skillet, liquify the butter over moderate heat. Mix in red bell pepper, carrots, celery, and onion; cook and mix for 5 minutes till onion becomes translucent and has softened. Mix in cooked pork, corn, Cheddar cheese, sour cream, cream of chicken soup, and noodles, then add black pepper and salt to

season. Turn mixture onto the prepped baking dish. Scatter the bread crumbs over top.

4. In the prepped oven, bake for 30 to 35 minutes till bubbly.

Per serving:

Calories: 382

Fat: 29.1g

Saturated Fat: 4.5g

Trans Fat: 24.6g

Carbohydrates: 1.7g

Fiber: 0.1g

Sodium: 954mg

Protein: 25g

83. Fast Miso Ramen

Prepare it in: *10 minutes*

Cook it in: *40 minutes*

Servings: *3*

Ingredients

- 6 oz. of noodles
- 2 tablespoons of miso paste
- 2 cloves of garlic
- 1 tablespoon of sambal oelek
- 2½ cups of vegetable broth

- 2 oz. of mung bean sprouts
- 4 small discs of roast pork (cooked)
- 4 surimi pieces
- 1 oz. of corn
- 2 seaweed leaves
- 2 spring onions
- Vegetable oil

Instructions

1. Cook the ramen noodles.

2. Heat the oil in the saucepan. Add garlic and sambal oelek. Before it turns brown, add the broth and stir in the miso paste.

3. Rinse the mung bean seedlings with water and put them briefly in the broth, as well as the roast pork and the surimi pieces, so that they become warm.

4. Cut the spring onions into small pieces.

5. Place the noodles in a large bowl. Arrange everything in a circle except the spring onions. Pour in the broth from the center (let it get hot again beforehand).

Finally, put the spring onions in the middle.

Per serving:

Calories: 382

Fat: 29.1g

Saturated Fat: 4.5g

Trans Fat: 24.6g

Carbohydrates: 1.7g

Fiber: 0.1g

Sodium: 954mg

Protein: 25g

84. Tonkotsu Ramen

Prepare it in: *10 minutes*

Cook it in: *40 minutes*

Servings: *3*

Ingredients

For the broth:

- 3 lbs. pork bones, with some meat
- 1 onion, peeled and halved
- 4 cloves garlic
- 1-inch ginger root, peeled

For the ramen:

- 8 cups Tonkotsu pork broth
- 12 oz. dried or fresh ramen noodles
- 12 slices Cha Shu pork slices
- 4 large ramen eggs
- 3 oz. dried shiitake ore enoki mushrooms, rehydrated
- 1/2 cup bamboo shoots, if desired
- 1/2 cup sweet corn, if desired
- 1/2 cup green onions, thinly sliced

For the miso tare:

- 1/2 cup Shiro miso
- 1/4 cup of sake
- 1/4 cup mirin
- 1 1/2 teaspoons kosher salt

Instructions

1. Add pork bones to a large stockpot and cover with cold water. Let sit for 12 hours.

2. Pour 2 cups of water into a large saucepan and bring to a boil over medium-high heat.

3. Meanwhile, transfer pork bones to a pot, cover them with boiling water, and set to sauté on High. Simmer for 10 minutes and press

cancel.

4. Drain water, place bones in a bowl of cold water, and then remove any fat. Clean the inner pot.

5. Add garlic, ginger, and onion, then return bones to the inner pot. Fill with water to the 3-4 fill line.

6. Lock the lid, set the valve to sealed. Cook on High pressure for 90 minutes (manual), then do a natural release.

7. Mix all ingredients for miso tare in a saucepan and simmer for 5 minutes on low heat.

8. Boil the ramen noodles per package instructions.

9. Rehydrate mushrooms in hot water until just softened. Drain mushrooms.

10. Heat oil in a nonstick skillet over medium heat. Brown pork slices on both sides.

11. Add 1/4 miso tare to each serving bowl. Add a ladle of tonkotsu broth, noodles and add another ladle of broth. Top with ramen egg, bamboo shoots, Cha Shu pork slices, sweet corn, and chopped green onion.

Per serving:

Calories 457

Fat 19.7 g

Carbohydrates 49.6 g

Sugar 7.5 g

Protein 56.6 g

Cholesterol 152 mg

85. Singapore Noodles

Prepare it in: *10 minutes*

Cook it in: *40 minutes*

Servings: *5*

Ingredients

- 1 pound Vermicelli pasta
- 4 cups water
- 2 breasts boneless chicken
- 2 pork chops
- 2 Garlic cloves
- 3 tablespoons oil
- ½ sliced onion

- 2 sliced carrots
- 2 celery stalks
- 12 ounces shrimps
- 1 cup bean sprouts
- 1 tablespoon soya sauce
- 3 tablespoons curry powder
- ¼ cup water

Instructions:

1. Boil water in a large pot and cook in the vermicelli pasta.
2. Drain and set aside.
3. Add oil into a pan and fry the chicken, pork, and garlic clove.
4. Now add in the sliced onion, sliced carrot, and fry till tender.
5. Add in the celery and the shrimps.
6. Mix in the bean sprouts, soya sauce, and curry powder.
7. Add in the water and let simmer for a few minutes.
8. Mix in the cooked pasta once the water has reduced.
9. Mix properly and serve!

Per serving:

Calories: 382

Fat: 29.1g

Saturated Fat: 4.5g

Trans Fat: 24.6g

Carbohydrates: 1.7g

Fiber: 0.1g

Sodium: 954mg

Protein: 25g

86. Asian Crab and Cucumber Salad

Prepare it in: 10 minutes

Cook it in: 40 minutes

Servings: 5

Ingredients

- 1 cucumber, sliced
- salt and ground black pepper to taste
- 1 (8 ounces) package imitation crabmeat, coarsely chopped
- 1 tablespoon white wine vinegar
- 1 tablespoon soy sauce

Direction

1. In a bowl put cucumber slices; season with pepper and salt. Toss imitation crab meat in.

2. In another bowl, whisk soy sauce and vinegar. Put in the crab and cucumber mixture. Toss till coated.

Per serving:

Calories: 382

Fat: 29.1g

Saturated Fat: 4.5g

Trans Fat: 24.6g

Carbohydrates: 1.7g

Fiber: 0.1g

Sodium: 954mg

Protein: 25g

87. Chilli Prawn Noodles

Prepare it in: *10 minutes*

Cook it in: *40 minutes*

Servings: *5*

Ingredients

- 1 lb. green (raw) prawns, unpeeled
- 2 tablespoons peanut oil
- 2½ cups chicken stock
- 1 clove garlic, crushed
- 2 tablespoons sweet chili sauce (e.g., Lingham's SOS brand)
- 4 tablespoons tomato sauce or ketchup
- ½ teaspoon salt
- 1 teaspoon sugar
- 1 teaspoon corn flour - dissolve in 1 tablespoon water
- 4 spring onions, chopped
- 1 egg white, beaten
- 14 oz. fresh Hokkien noodles

Instructions

1. Devein prawns by hooking out the black intestinal tract with a fine bamboo skewer. Heat the oil and cook the prawns until they become red, around 1 to 2 minutes. Simmer for 1 minute after adding the chicken stock. Garlic, chili sauce, tomato sauce, salt, and sugar are added to the pan. Mix thoroughly.

2. Add cornflour paste, bring to boil. Stir for 60 seconds. Add half the spring onion and toss well. Slowly dribble egg white into the sauce

(a good trick is to pour it through the tines of a fork), stirring constantly, until the sauce thickens.

3. Pour boiling water over noodles in a heatproof bowl, leave to stand for 2 minutes, and drain. Arrange on a serving platter and pour prawns and sauce on top. Scatter with remaining spring onion.

Per serving:

Calories: 434

Fat: 35.3g

Carbs: 10.5g

Protein: 18.4g

88. Seafood Shio ramen

Prepare it in: *10 minutes*

Cook it in: *40 minutes*

Servings: 3

Ingredients

- 6 oz. of glass noodles
- 2 cups of chicken broth
- 4 shiitake mushrooms

- 4 oz. of cod fillet
- 6 king prawns
- 3.5 oz. of tofu
- 1 carrot (preferably thin)
- 4.5 oz. of Chinese cabbage
- 1 spring onion
- 1 tablespoon of sherry (dry)
- 2 tablespoons of soy sauce
- ½ tablespoon of lemon juice
- Cayenne pepper

Instructions

1. Cut the glass noodles into 4-inch pieces, scald them with boiling water, let them steep for 2 minutes, and drain.

2. Clean the mushrooms and cut lengthwise into quarters. Rinse fish fillet briefly, pat dry, and cut into bite-size pieces. Remove the shell from the shrimp, leave the tailpieces on and gut them.

3. Cut the drained tofu into 8 cubes. Peel the carrot and slice it into thin slices. Clean, wash, halve and cut Chinese cabbage into strips of about 1 inch wide. Clean the

spring onion and slice it into thin slices.

4. Bring the broth to a boil. Add all the ingredients except the onions and let cook for 2 minutes.

5. Finally, season with sherry, soy sauce, lemon juice, and cayenne pepper and sprinkle with the spring onions.

Per serving:

Calories: 382

Fat: 29.1g

Saturated Fat: 4.5g

Trans Fat: 24.6g

Carbohydrates: 1.7g

Fiber: 0.1g

Sodium: 954mg

Protein: 25g

89. Roasted Cornish Hen

Prep Time: 15 mins

Cook it in: 1 hour

Servings: 8

Ingredients:

1 tablespoon dried basil, crushed

2 tablespoons lemon pepper

1 tablespoon poultry seasoning

Salt, to taste

4 (1½-pound) Cornish game hens, rinsed and dried completely

2 tablespoons butter, melted

Instructions:

1. Preheat the oven to 375 degrees F. Arrange lightly greased racks in 2 large roasting pans.

2. In a bowl, add the basil, lemon pepper, poultry seasoning and salt and mix well.

3. Coat each hen with melted butter and then rub with the seasoning mixture.

4. Arrange the hens into prepared roasting pans.

5. Roast for about 1 hour.

6. Remove the hens from the oven and place onto a cutting board.

7. With a piece of foil, cover each hen loosely for about 10 minutes before carving.

8. Cut into desired sized pieces and

serve.

Per serving:

Calories: 739

Fat: 51.8g

Saturated Fat: 14.1g

Trans Fat: 37.7g

Carbohydrates: 3.9g

Fiber: 1.2g

Sodium: 234mg

Protein: 57.8g

90. Prime Rib Roast

Prep Time: 15 mins

Cook it in: 1 hour 25 minutes

Servings: 15

Ingredients:

10 garlic cloves, minced

2 teaspoons dried thyme, crushed

2 tablespoons butter, melted

Salt and freshly ground black pepper, to taste

1 (10-pound) prime rib roast

Instructions:

1. In a bowl, add the garlic, thyme, butter, salt and black pepper and mix until well combined.

2. Coat the rib with garlic mixture and arrange in a large roasting pan, fatty side up.

3. Set aside to marinate at room temperature for at least 1 hour.

4. Preheat the oven to 500 degrees F.

5. Place the roasting pan into the oven and roast for about 20 minutes.

6. Now, reduce the temperature to 325 degrees F and roast for about 65-75 minutes.

7. Remove from the oven and place the rib roast onto a cutting board for about 10-15 minutes before slicing.

8. With a sharp knife, cut the rib roast into desired size slices and serve.

Per serving:

Calories: 499

Fat: 25.9g

Saturated Fat: 9.6g

Trans Fat: 16.3g

Carbohydrates: 0.7g

Fiber: 0.1g

Sodium: 199mg

Protein: 61.5g

91. Katsu Curry Ramen

Prepare it in: *10 minutes*

Cook it in: *40 minutes*

Servings: *3*

Ingredients

- 2 lbs. pork feet
- 2 lbs. pork neck bones
- 2 lbs. pork leg bones
- 2 chicken backbones
- 6 cloves garlic
- 1 cup dried shiitake mushrooms, ground
- 1/4 cup bonito flakes
- 1 3-inch piece ginger
- 1 onion, cut into thirds
- 1 leek, halved lengthwise, sliced crosswise, and rinsed
- 1/4 cup dried anchovy
- 1/4 sheet kombu
- 2 tablespoons salt
- 1 tablespoon sugar
- 2 cubes curry bouillon
- 1 teaspoon fish powder

For the pork katsu:

- 1 egg
- 1 lb. pork loin, sliced into 4 portions
- 1 cup all-purpose flour
- 1 gallon of vegetable oil, for deep-frying
- salt, to taste
- 2 cups panko bread crumbs

For the toppings:

- 4 ramen eggs, halved
- 4 portions fresh ramen noodles
- 1 green onion, chopped
- 2 tablespoons toasted sesame seeds

Instructions

1. Place pork feet and all bones in a large stockpot and cover them with water. Cover with lid and bring to a boil. After 10 minutes, remove from heat and strain the bones. Clean bones under running water. Return cleaned bones into a rinsed stockpot,

cover with water and bring to a boil again.

2. Char leek, ginger, garlic, and onion in a skillet until almost burnt. Set aside.

3. Add charred vegetables, bonito flakes, anchovy, ground mushrooms, and kombu to the pot with the bones. Let it boil for 6 hours on low heat. Boil for 12 hours more, then add some salt, sugar, and fish powder. Simmer for 6 hours on low heat. Strain the stock and back it to the pot.

4. Then, add 2 quarts of pork broth and curry bouillon to make curry broth. Let it boil and whisk well.

5. Add oil to a heavy-bottomed pot to 350ºF. Tenderize pork loin pieces with the flat end of a meat mallet and salt it. Beat egg and 1 tablespoon water together to create an egg wash. Dredge each portion in flour, then egg wash, then bread crumbs. Fry pork loin for 4-5 minutes or so until golden brown and cooked through. Remove from the pan and let it rest for 1-2 minutes.

6. Cook noodles following the recipe or package Instructions, drain, and place in bowls.

7. Pour hot curry broth over noodles and top with fried pork katsu and halved ramen egg. Sprinkle with sesame seeds, chopped green onions, and serve.

Per serving:

Calories 829

Total fat 46g

Total carbs 4g

Protein 86g

Sodium: 181mg

92. Long–Life Noodles

Prepare it in: 10 minutes

Cook it in: 20 minutes

Servings: 3

Ingredients

- 4 spring onions
- 8 dried shiitake mushrooms, soaked

- 1 large e-fu noodle cake, about 11 oz.
- 2 tablespoon soy sauce
- 1 tablespoon oyster sauce
- 1 teaspoon sesame oil
- 1 teaspoon sugar
- ¾ cup chicken stock
- 1 tablespoon peanut oil
- 1 tablespoon grated ginger
- 2 cloves garlic, crushed

Instructions

1. Finely slice the green tops of the spring onions and reserve. Cut the remainder into matchsticks. Drain mushrooms, discard stems, and slice caps finely.
2. Cook noodles in boiling water for 3 to 4 minutes. Rinse in cold water and drain well.
3. Mix soy sauce, oyster sauce, sesame oil, sugar, and chicken stock in a bowl and set aside.
4. Heat oil and stir fry the ginger and garlic for 1 minute. Add spring onion matchsticks, all the mushrooms, and sauce

ingredients and bring to a boil, stirring. Cook for 1 minute.

5. Add noodles and cook for about 2 minutes, or until they have absorbed most of the sauce.
6. Serve immediately, scattered with the spring onion greens.

Per serving:

Calories: 739

Fat: 51.8g

Saturated Fat: 14.1g

Trans Fat: 37.7g

Carbohydrates: 3.9g

Fiber: 1.2g

Sodium: 234mg

Protein: 57.8g

93. Shrimp Garlic Ramen

Prepare it in: *10 minutes*

Cook it in: *20 minutes*

Servings: *3*

Ingredients

- 4 eggs ramen eggs, halved
- 2 tablespoons avocado oil

- 4 cloves garlic, chopped
- 1 tablespoon ginger, grated
- 2 tablespoons red curry paste
- 4 cups chicken broth
- 1 (13.5 oz.) can coconut milk
- 1 tablespoon fish sauce
- 1 lb. crab clusters
- 2 portions ramen noodles
- 1 lb. shrimp, tails removed, peeled, and deveined
- Kosher salt and pepper, to taste
- 4 lime wedges
- 1 bunch cilantro, chopped
- 1 bunch green onion, chopped

Instructions

1. Cook ginger and garlic in a hot oiled pan for 2 minutes, until translucent. Add curry paste and fry for 1 minute more. Pour in coconut milk, broth, and fish sauce. Stir well until combined. Set heat to medium-high, and add crab meat to the pot. Boil for 3-5 minutes.

2. While the crab is boiling, cook noodles according to the manufacturer's Instructions in another pot. Drain and rinse, set aside.

3. Add shrimp to the broth and boil for 2-3 minutes, until cooked. Add salt and pepper.

4. Divide broth, noodles, and seafood into separate bowls. Top each bowl with egg halves and chopped cilantro and green onions.

- 6 oz. rice noodles
- 3 tablespoons soya sauce
- 2 tablespoons lemon juice
- 2 teaspoons honey
- 1 teaspoon cornstarch
- 1 tablespoon ginger
- 2 tablespoons oil
- 3 stalks of celery
- 2 bell peppers
- 2 garlic cloves
- 1 can water chestnuts
- 1 lb. sirloin steak
- A pinch of black pepper
- 1 cup edamame
- ¼ cup water

Instructions

1. Cook noodles according to the instructions on the package.
2. In a bowl add the soya sauce, lemon juice, honey, cornstarch, and ¼ cup of water.
3. Add in the ginger.
4. Heat oil in a pan and stir fry the celery and the peppers.
5. Add in the garlic and the chestnuts and fry.
6. Heat oil in another pan and add in the sirloin steak, season with black pepper.
7. Add the soya sauce mixture.
8. Let it cook.
9. Add in the edamame and the bell peppers and let cook for a few minutes.
10. Serve with rice noodles!

Per serving:

Calories 829

Total fat 46g

Total carbs 4g

Protein 86g

Sodium: 181mg

94. German Spaghettini

Prepare it in: *10 minutes*

Cook it in: *20 minutes*

Servings: *3*

Ingredients

- 1 pound beef
- ¼ cup Italian sausage
- 6 bacon slices
- 15 ounces tomato sauce
- 28 ounces canned tomatoes
- 1/3 cup sugar
- 12 ounces spaghettini
- 2 tablespoons oil

Instructions

1. Boil the spaghettini in a large saucepan filled with water.
2. Drain and set aside.
3. Add oil into a frying pan and fry the ground beef until it is cooked.
4. Remove from heat and now fry the sausage in the frying pan.
5. Now add in the cooked beef.
6. Add in the bacon slices, tomato sauce, tomatoes, and canned tomatoes.

7. Let it cook for 40 minutes.

8. Now mix in the cooked Spaghettini in the tomato mixture.

9. Pour this in a baking rectangular dish.

10. Preheat your oven to 300 degrees Fahrenheit.

11. Put this baking dish in the preheated oven to bake for 30 minutes.

12. Serve!

   Per serving:

   Calories: 739

   Fat: 51.8g

   Saturated Fat: 14.1g

   Trans Fat: 37.7g

   Carbohydrates: 3.9g

   Fiber: 1.2g

   Sodium: 234mg

   Protein: 57.8g

95. Carnivore Beef Stew

Prep Time: 20 min

Cook it in: 8 hours

Servings: 8

Ingredients:

2 pounds chuck roast, cubed

2 pounds beef marrow bones

2 tablespoons beef tallow

8 ounce mushrooms, quartered

2 teaspoons dried thyme

1 teaspoon ground black pepper

6 cups bone broth

4 garlic cloves, minced

2 teaspoons salt

Instructions:

1. Put tallow and meat in a skillet and cook for about 4 minutes on each side.

2. Put the marrow bones in the slow cooker and stir in the seared meat.

3. Mix well and add the rest of the ingredients.

4. Secure the lid and cook for about 8 hours on LOW.

5. Dish out in a bowl and serve hot.

   Per serving:

   Calories: 509

Fat: 20.7g

Saturated Fat: 8.8g

Carbohydrates: 2.1g

Fiber: 1.2g

Sodium: 884mg

Protein: 75.5g

96. Turkey Salsa Meatloaf

*Prepare & **Cook it in**: 1hr & 15 mins*

Servings: *5*

Ingredients

- 2 Eggs
- 1 Cup Oats
- 1 Onion, Minced
- 3/4 Cup Grated Carrot
- 1 1/2 Teaspoons Worcestershire Sauce
- 1/2 Teaspoon Salt
- 2 Teaspoons Garlic Powder
- 1/2 Teaspoon Dried Thyme
- 1 Lb Ground Turkey
- 1/2 Cup Salsa

Cooking Instructions

1. Mix everything together but don't add the salsa & from into a loaf; put in the oven at 175C/350F approximately40 mins.

2. Remove the loaf from the oven; cover with salsa &bake until done, approximately half an hour more.

Per serving:

Calories: 382

Fat: 29.1g

Saturated Fat: 4.5g

Trans Fat: 24.6g

Carbohydrates: 1.7g

Fiber: 0.1g

Sodium: 954mg

Protein: 25g

97. Shredded Beef Tongue

Prep Time: 5 min

Cook it in: 15 min

Servings: 6

Ingredients:

1 teaspoon real salt

2 pounds beef tongue, grass-fed

4 bay leaves

Instructions:

1. Put the beef tongue in the crockpot and sprinkle salt in it.

2. Add the bay leaves and water enough to cover the beef tongue.

3. Cover the lid and cook on LOW for about 8 hours.

4. Shred the beef and dish out to serve warm.

   Per serving:

   Calories: 432

   Fat: 33.8g

   Saturated Fat: 12.3g

   Carbohydrates: 0.5g

   Fiber: 0.2g

   Sodium: 486mg

   Protein: 29.2g

98. Deli Style Roast Beef

Prep Time: 10 min

Cook it in: 20 min

Servings: 4

Ingredients:

1 (2 pounds) eye of round roast

1 tablespoon Hey Grill Hey Signature Beef Seasoning

Instructions:

1. Foreheat the grill to medium-high and grease the grill grates.

2. Sprinkle the beef seasoning on all sides of the eye of the round roast.

3. Arrange the roast on the grill grates and cook for about 20 minutes.

4. Remove from the grill and slice to serve.

   Per serving:

   Calories: 321

   Fat: 11g

   Saturated Fat: 4g

   Carbohydrates: 1g

   Fiber: 1g

   Sodium: 127mg

   Protein: 50g

99. Easy Seared Tongue

Prep Time: 25 min

Cook it in: 2 hours 16 min

Servings: 2

Ingredients:

4 marrow bones, canoe cut

1 beef tongue

1 tablespoon lard

Salt, to taste

Instructions:

1. Put the beef tongue in salted water and refrigerate overnight.

2. Rinse the beef tongue and boil on low heat for about 2 hours.

3. Peel the tongue and arrange the marrow bones on a baking sheet.

4. Transfer the baking sheet into the broiler and broil for about 10 minutes.

5. Put the lard and beef tongue slices over medium heat in a pan and sear for about 3 minutes on each side.

6. Dish out and serve warm with the broiled bone marrows.

Per serving:

Calories: 464

Fat: 29.9g

Saturated Fat: 12.6g

Carbohydrates: 0.6g

Fiber: 1.2g

Sodium: 305mg

Protein: 47g

100.   Slow Cooker Beef Heart

Prep Time: 10 min

Cook it in: 7 hours

Servings: 4

Ingredients:

6 garlic cloves

2 pounds beef heart, grass-fed

1 cup beef bone broth

2 tablespoons pink Himalayan salt

Instructions:

1. Season the beef heart with salt and add to the slow cooker.

2. Stir in the garlic and beef bone broth and cover the lid.

3. Cook for about 7 hours on LOW and dish out to serve hot.

Per serving:

Calories: 391

Fat: 11g

Saturated Fat: 3.4g

Carbohydrates: 3.1g

Fiber: 0.3g

Sodium: 3200mg

Protein: 66.4g

101. Grilled Beef Heart

Prep Time: 15 min

Cook it in: 12 min

Servings: 4

Ingredients:

½ cup balsamic vinegar

1 (2 pounds) beef heart

Salt and pepper, to taste

2 tablespoons tallow

Instructions:

1. Marinate the beef heart in the balsamic vinegar overnight.
2. Pat the heart dries and season generously with salt and pepper.
3. Heat tallow in a skillet on medium heat and add the beef

heart.

4. Cook for 6 minutes on both sides and dish out to serve hot.

Per serving:

Calories: 438

Fat: 17.1g

Saturated Fat: 6.4g

Carbohydrates: 0.6g

Fiber: 0g

Sodium: 135mg

Protein: 64.6g

102. Roasted Bone Marrow

Prep Time: 15 min

Cook it in: 20 min

Servings: 1

Ingredients:

4 bone marrow halves

Salt and pepper, to taste

Instructions:

1. Foreheat the oven to 350 degrees F and line a baking tray with foil.
2. Arrange the bone marrow halves on the baking tray and transfer it

into the oven.

3. Bake for about 20 minutes and take out from the oven to serve hot.

Per serving:

Calories: 286

Fat: 14g

Saturated Fat: 6.6g

Carbohydrates: 0.7g

Fiber: 1.2g

Sodium: 200mg

Protein: 38.8g

103.   Liver Meatballs

Prep Time: 15 min

Cook it in: 12 min

Servings: 6

Ingredients:

2 pounds ground beef

1 pound ground liver

4 tablespoons rosemary

1 tablespoon chili pepper flakes

2 tablespoons basil

1 teaspoon mixed pepper

Instructions:

1. Heat the oven to 375 degrees F.

2. Combine beef and liver with all

3. other ingredients in a bowl and mix well.

4. Form meatballs out of this mixture and arrange on the baking tray.

5. Place in the oven and bake for about 12 minutes.

6. Dish out in a platter and serve warm.

Per serving:

Calories: 399

Fat: 12.6g

Saturated Fat: 4.4g

Carbohydrates: 5g

Fiber: 1.5g

Sodium: 167mg

Protein: 60.8g

Snacks

104. Carnivore French Fries

Prep Time: 10 min

Cook it in: 23 min

Servings: 1

Ingredients:

10g pork rinds

¼ teaspoon salt

4 oz. chicken, cooked

1 whole egg

Instructions:

1. Foreheat the oven to 350 degrees F and line a parchment paper in the baking dish.

2. Pour chicken with all other ingredients in a blender and blend until smooth.

3. Stuff this mixture in the plastic bag and cut a small hole at one end.

4. Pipe out the fries on the baking dish and transfer it into the oven.

5. Bake for about 20 minutes and broil for 3 minutes on high.

6. Parcel out in a platter and serve hot.

Per serving:

Calories: 291

Fat: 11.4g

Saturated Fat: 3.8g

Carbohydrates: 0.3g

Fiber: 0g

Sodium: 907mg

Protein: 44.8g

105. Meatloaf With Raisins

Prepare & ***Cook it in****: 1hr & 25 mins*

Servings: *16*

Ingredients

- 2 Lbs Lean Ground Beef
- 2 Cups Crushed Wheat Flakes
- 4 Eggs, Room Temperature, Slightly Beaten
- 1 Teaspoon Salt
- 1/2 Teaspoon Pepper

- 1 Cup Milk
- 3/4 Cup Catsup
- 2 Teaspoons Worcestershire Sauce
- 2 Cups Raisins
- 1 Medium Onion, Diced

Cooking Instructions

1. Preheat the oven at 350 F/175 C.
2. Mix together everything & shape into a shallow dome in a baking dish with sides (10 inch round).
3. Bake for a minimum period of one hour &15 minutes.

Per serving:

Calories: 321

Fat: 11g

Saturated Fat: 4g

Carbohydrates: 1g

Fiber: 1g

Sodium: 127mg

Protein: 50g

106. Grilled Bone Marrow with Garlic Parmesan Crust

Prep Time: 10 min

Cook it in: 15 min

Servings: 4

Ingredients:

½ cup parsley, chopped

4 beef marrow bones, cut lengthwise

4 garlic cloves, minced

Salt and pepper, to taste

⅓ cup olive oil

¼ cup parmesan cheese, grated

Instructions:

1. Foreheat the grill to medium-high and grease the grill grates.
2. Combine garlic, parsley, olive oil, salt, and pepper in a bowl.
3. Decant this mixture over the top of the beef marrow bones and top with parmesan cheese.
4. Transfer to the grill and cook for about 10 minutes.
5. Remove from the grill and serve hot.

Per serving:

Calories: 210

Fat: 20.1g

Saturated Fat: 4.2g

Carbohydrates: 1.8g

Fiber: 0.5g

Sodium: 95mg

Protein: 7.5g

107.   Steak Nuggets

Prep Time: 10 min

Cook it in: 6 min

Servings: 2

Ingredients:

1 large egg, organic pasture-raised

1 pound venison steak, cut into chunks

Lard, for frying

½ cup pork panko

½ cup parmesan cheese, grated

½ teaspoon homemade seasoned salt

Instructions:

1. Mix pork panko with salt and cheese in a bowl and whisk the egg in another bowl.

2. Dip the steak chunks in the egg, then dredge in the breading mixture.

3. Freeze the steak chunks for about 3 hours.

4. Heat lard and add steak chunks.

5. Fry for about 3 minutes and dish out to serve.

Per serving:

Calories: 350

Fat: 20g

Saturated Fat: 6g

Carbohydrates: 1g

Fiber: 0g

Sodium: 335mg

Protein: 40g

108.   Organ Meat Pie

Prep Time: 5 min

Cook it in: 20 min

Servings: 3

Ingredients:

½ pound ground beef heart

½ pound ground beef

½ pound ground beef liver

3 eggs

2 tablespoons beef tallow

Salt, to taste

Instructions:

1. Foreheat the oven to 350 degrees F and grease a 9-inch pie plate.

2. Combine ground beef with the rest of the ingredients in a bowl.

3. Decant the beef mixture into the pie plate and transfer it in the oven.

4. Bake for about 20 minutes and remove from the oven to serve.

Per serving:

Calories: 412

Fat: 28g

Saturated Fat: 10g

Carbohydrates: 2g

Fiber: 0g

Sodium: 162mg

Protein: 35g

109.　Cheddar Meatloaf

Prepare & ***Cook it in****: 2 hrs& 10 mins*

Servings: *7*

Ingredients:-

- 2 Lbs Ground Beef
- 1 1/2 Cups Italian Breadcrumbs (Or Plain)
- 0.75 (16 Ounce) Jar Mild Salsa
- 1/4 Cup Ketchup
- 1/2 Cup Cheddar Cheese Or 1/2 Cup Mozzarella Cheese, Small Diced
- 2 Dashes Basil
- 2 Dashes Oregano
- 2 Dashes Onion Powder
- 2 Dashes Garlic Powder
- 1 Pinch Salt
- 1 Pinch Pepper
- 1 Egg
- Shredded Cheese, For The Top

Cooking Instructions :-

1. Mix together everything but don't mix the shredded cheese.

2. Shape the mixture into a loaf pan.

3. Spread a small layer of ketchup over the top.

4. Bake at 190C/375 F approximately 1 hr and 30 minutes, top with cheese. Bake again until cheese completely

melts. Cover the top with foil, if looks too cooked and decrease the heat to 175C/350F.

Per serving:

Calories 829

Total fat 46g

Total carbs 4g

Protein 86g

Sodium: 181mg

110.   Cheesy Air Fryer Meatballs

Prep Time: 20 min

Cook it in: 12 min

Servings: 6

Ingredients:

2 large pastured eggs

2 pounds grass-fed ground beef

2-ounces pork rinds

1 teaspoon pink sea salt

3-ounces Italian cheese blend, shredded

1 tablespoon lard

Instructions:

1. Foreheat the Air Fryer to 350 degrees F.

2. Combine ground beef with all other ingredients in a bowl and knead well.

3. Form small balls out of this mixture and place it in the fryer basket.

4. Cook for about 12 minutes, flipping once in between.

5. Take out from the Air fryer and serve warm.

Per serving:

Calories:419

Fat: 26.1g

Saturated Fat: 11.4g

Carbohydrates: 0.6g

Fiber: 0g

Sodium: 752mg

Protein: 42.5g

111.   Carnivore Taco Pie

Prep Time: 20 min

Cook it in: 30 min

Servings: 8

Ingredients:

3 tablespoons taco seasoning

6 eggs

1 pound ground beef

1 cup heavy cream

1 cup cheese, shredded

Instructions:

1. Foreheat the oven to 350 degrees F and grease a pie pan lightly.

2. Cook the ground beef for about 5 minutes in a skillet until browned.

3. Sprinkle with taco seasoning and mix well.

4. Stir the heavy cream with eggs in a bowl and mix well.

5. Place the beef in the pie pan and top with half of the cheese.

6. Add the egg-cream mixture and top with the remaining cheese.

7. Shift into the oven and bake for about 30 minutes.

8. Remove from the oven and serve warm.

Per serving:

Calories: 353

Fat: 30g

Saturated Fat: 15g

Carbohydrates: 2g

Fiber: 1g

Sodium: 264mg

Protein: 18g

112. Carnivore Cake

Prep Time: 15 min

Cook it in: 2 hours

Servings: 14

Ingredients:

½ pound pork shoulder, chopped

1¼ pounds pork liver, chopped

¾ pound pork back fat, chopped

4 hard-boiled eggs

3 teaspoons Redmond Real Salt

TOPPINGS:

12 slices bacon

12 slices of prosciutto

Instructions:

1. Foreheat the oven to 300 degrees F and grease a 7-inch cake pan.

2. Put the pork shoulder, pork liver, and pork back fat in a food processor and puree until

smooth.

3. Put the pork mixture in the cake pan and tightly cover with foil.

4. Pour the boiling water into a roasting pan and insert the cake pan.

5. Shift into the oven and bake for about 2 hours.

6. Insert 4 egg-sized holes in the meat with a spoon and add the eggs in these holes.

7. Cover the eggs with the meat from the pan and refrigerate for 2 hours.

8. Fold the prosciutto around the cake and make bacon roses.

9. Place the bacon roses on the cake and serve to enjoy it.

Per serving:

Calories: 441

Fat: 34.1g

Saturated Fat: 12.1g

Carbohydrates: 1.9g

Fiber: 0g

Sodium: 1299mg

Protein: 27.5g

113. Meatloaf Barbecue Style

*Prepare & **Cook it in**: 1 hr& 30 mins*

Servings: *6*

Ingredients:

- 1 1/2 lbs ground beef
- 1/2 cup fresh breadcrumb
- 1 onion, finely chopped
- 1 egg, beaten
- 1 1/2 teaspoons salt
- 1 (8 ounce) can tomato sauce
- 1/4 teaspoon pepper
- 1/2 cup water
- 3 tablespoons brown sugar
- 2 tablespoons prepared mustard
- 2 teaspoons Worcestershire sauce

Cooking Instructions:

1. Combine the crumbs, beef, egg, onion, pepper, salt and half can of tomato sauce together.

2. Shape into loaf & place the loaf into a loaf pan.

3. Combine all of the leftover ingredients and transfer the mixture over the loaf.

4. Bake in 175C/350F oven approximately 1 hour &and 15 minutes.

Per serving:

Calories: 321

Fat: 11g

Saturated Fat: 4g

Carbohydrates: 1g

Fiber: 1g

Sodium: 127mg

Protein: 50g

114.   Herb Roasted Bone Marrow

Prep Time: 5 min

Cook it in: 15 min

Servings: 1

Ingredients:

1 tablespoon fresh rosemary

2 beef marrow bones, grass-fed/pasture-raised

1 tablespoon fresh thyme

Salt and black pepper, to taste

Instructions:

1. Foreheat the oven to 400 degrees F and grease a baking dish.

2. Arrange the bone marrows on the baking dish and season with salt, pepper, thyme, and rosemary.

3. Shift into the oven and bake for about 15 minutes.

4. Dish out in a platter and serve warm.

Per serving:

Calories: 305

Fat: 14.7g

Saturated Fat: 6.9g

Carbohydrates: 4.5g

Fiber: 3.6g

Sodium: 203mg

Protein: 39.2g

 Tomato Pork Paste

Prepare it in: 5-8 minutes

Cook it in: 15 minutes

Servings: 4

Ingredients:

- 2 cups tomato puree
- 1 tablespoon red wine

- 1-pound lean ground pork
- 8-10-ounce pack paste of your choice, uncooked
- Salt and black pepper to taste
- 1 tablespoon vegetable oil

Instructions:

1. Season the pork with black pepper and salt.

2. Place your instant pot over a dry kitchen platform. Open the top lid and plug it on.

3. Press "SAUTE" Cooking function; add the oil and heat it.

4. In the pot, add the ground meat; stir-cook using wooden spatula until turns evenly brown for 8-10 minutes.

5. Add the wine. Cook for 1-2 minutes.

6. Add the ingredients; gently stir to mix well.

7. Properly close the top lid; make sure that the safety valve is properly locked.

8. Press "MEAT/STEW" Cooking function; set pressure level to "HIGH" and set the **Cook it in** to 6 minutes.

9. Allow the pressure to build to cook the ingredients.

10. After **Cook it in** is over press "CANCEL" setting. Find and press "NPR" Cooking function. This setting is for the natural release of inside pressure, and it takes around 10 minutes to slowly release pressure.

11. Slowly open the lid, take out the cooked recipe in serving containers. Serve warm.

Per serving:

Calories: 382

Fat: 29.1g

Saturated Fat: 4.5g

Trans Fat: 24.6g

Carbohydrates: 1.7g

Fiber: 0.1g

Sodium: 954mg

Protein: 25g

115. Garlic Pulled Pork

Prepare it in: 5 minutes

Cook it in: 1 hour and 40 minutes

Servings: 12

Ingredients:

- 4-pounds pork shoulder, boneless and cut into 3 pieces
- 2 tablespoons soy sauce
- 2 tablespoons brown sugar
- 1 cup chicken broth
- 10 cloves garlic, finely chopped
- 2 tablespoons butter, melted at room temperature

Instructions:

1. In a mixing bowl, combine the broth, soy sauce, and brown sugar. Add the garlic and stir to combine.

2. Preheat your instant pot using the sauté setting and add the butter.

3. When warmed, add the pork pieces and stir-cook until browned on all sides.

4. Add the soy mix; stir gently.

5. Seal the lid and cook on high pressure for 90 minutes using the manual setting.

6. Let the pressure release naturally, about 10 minutes.

7. Uncover the instant pot; take out the meat and shred it using a fork.

8. Return the shredded meat to the instant pot and stir the mixture well.

Transfer to serving plates and serve.

Per serving:

Calories: 142

Protein: 11.2 g

Fat: 8.2 g

Carbohydrates: 3.5 g

116.   Buttered Pork Chops

Prepare it in: 15 minutes

Cook it in: 15 minutes

Servings: 4

Ingredients:

- Pork Chops (4)

- Salt (1 t.)
- Bacon Grease (2 T.)
- Butter (4 T.)
- Pepper (1 t.)

Instructions:

1. If you are looking for a quick and easy meal, look no further than buttered pork chops! Within twenty minutes, you'll be sitting down and enjoying your meal. You will want to start off this recipe by taking out your pork chops and seasoning them on either side. If you need more than a teaspoon of salt and pepper, feel free to season as desired.

2. Next, you are going to want to place your skillet over high heat and place the bacon grease and butter into the bottom.

3. Once the butter is melted and the grease is sizzling, pop the pork chops into the skillet and sear on either side for three to four minutes. In the end, the pork should be a nice golden color.

4. When the meat is cooked as desired, remove the skillet from the heat and enjoy your meal!

Per serving:

Calories: 450

Fats: 30g

Proteins: 45g

117.   Quick and Easy Pork Loin Roast

Prepare it in: 45 minutes

Cook it in: 30 minutes

Servings: 6

Ingredients:

- Bacon Grease (1 T.)
- Salt (1 t.)
- Pork Loin (3 Lbs.)
- Pepper (1 t.)

Instructions:

1. Even with just four ingredients, you will be surprised how delicious this recipe will be! Before you start cooking, you will want to go ahead and heat your oven to 375 degrees.

2. As the oven is warming up, take out your baking pan and gently place the pork loin into the bottom. Once in place, go ahead and rub the salt and pepper all over the sides. Be sure that each side is coated to help even out the flavor over the loin.

3. Finally, pop the dish into the oven for one hour. At the end of this time, the meat should be cooked through to your liking. Remember that you will want your meat to be slightly rare to get the most nutrients from it.

4. Remove the meat from the oven, allow it to cool for several minutes, and then your meat is ready to be enjoyed.

Per serving:

Calories: 520

Fats: 35g

Protein: 50g

118. Cheese and Ham Roll-ups

Prepare it in: 20 minutes

Cook it in: 15 minutes

Servings: 7

Ingredients:

- Eggs (2)
- Ham, Diced (1 C.)
- Cheddar Cheese, Shredded (.50 C.)
- Mozzarella Cheese, Shredded (.75 C.)
- Parmesan Cheese (.50 C.)

Instructions:

1. If you ever find yourself craving a snack while following the Carnivore Diet, this little recipe should do the trick! Start off by heating your oven to 375 degrees.

2. As the oven warms up, take out a mixing bowl and combine the egg and shredded cheeses together. Once the clumps are taken out, you can also add in the ham and give everything a good stir.

3. Now, you will want to take out a baking sheet and line it with parchment paper. When this is in

place, divide your mixture onto the parchment paper for six or eight rolls.

4. When you are ready, place it into the oven and cook these for about twenty minutes. By the end, the cheese should create a brown crust.

5. If it looks like this, remove it from the oven, allow the roll-ups to cool, and enjoy your quick and easy snack!

Per serving:

Calories: 200

Fats: 15g

Proteins: 15g

119.   Meat Cup Snacks

Prepare it in: 25 minutes

Cook it in: 15 minutes

Servings: 4

Ingredients:

- Eggs (6)
- Ham (6 Slices)

- Pepper (1 t.)
- Shredded Cheddar Cheese (.50 C.)

Instructions:

1. Looking for another great snack? These will be perfect for breakfast, lunch, or dinner! Start off by heating the oven to 375 degrees. As it warms up, you can prep for this recipe by taking out a muffin tin and greasing it up with butter or bacon grease. If you want to avoid a mess, you can also use silicone muffin tins.

2. Once you are ready, take your slices of ham and line each hole with them, carefully placing them into a bottom.

3. When the ham is in place, get out a skillet and scramble the six eggs until they reach the desired consistency. Once cooked through, go ahead and scoop the scrambled egg into the muffin tin and place it on top of the ham.

4. For a final touch, sprinkle the egg with some shredded cheddar

cheese. At this point, feel free to season these cups with salt and pepper. If not, they are going to taste delicious without any seasoning!

5. Finally, pop the muffin tin into your oven for about ten minutes. At the end of this time, the cheese should be melted and a nice golden color. If it looks like this, remove from the oven, allow to cool, and enjoy!

Per serving:

Calories: 250

Fats: 15g

Proteins: 20g

120. Pork and Cheese Stuffed Peppers

Prepare it in: 30 minutes

Cook it in: 25 minutes

Servings: 2

Ingredients:

- 2 sweet Italian peppers, deveined and halved
- 1/2 Spanish onion, finely chopped
- 1 cup marinara sauce
- 1/2 cup cheddar cheese, grated
- 4 ounces pork, ground

Instructions:

1. Heat 1 tablespoon of canola oil in a saucepan over a moderate heat. Then, sauté the onion for 3 to 4 minutes until tender and fragrant.

2. Add in the ground pork; cook for 3 to 4 minutes more. Add in Italian seasoning mix. Spoon the mixture into the pepper halves.

3. Spoon the marinara sauce into a lightly greased baking dish. Arrange the stuffed peppers in the baking dish.

4. Bake in the preheated oven at 395 degrees F for 17 to 20 minutes. Top with cheddar cheese and continue to bake for about 5 minutes or until the top is golden brown. Bon appétit!

Per serving:

Calories: 291

Fat: 11.4g

Saturated Fat: 3.8g

Carbohydrates: 0.3g

Fiber: 0g

Sodium: 907mg

Protein: 44.8g Peppered Pork Rack

Prepare it in: 120 minutes

Cook it in: 1 hour and 30 minutes

Servings: 6

Ingredients:

- Pepper (.25 C.)
- Pork Rib Rack (1)

Instructions:

1. While simple, this peppered pork rack can become a staple in your new carnivore diet because it is easy to make and delicious! You'll want to start off by heating your oven only to 375 degrees.

2. As the oven warms up, you will want to prepare your rib rack. Be sure that you coat the roast with the pepper seasoning. While a quarter of a cup of pepper may seem like a lot, you will want this much for maximum flavor.

3. When the meat is coated, place the roast into a baking dish, bones up. If you are ready to cook your meal, pop it into the oven for one hour and thirty minutes. Once it is cooked through, you can remove it from the oven and allow it to rest for around ten minutes.

4. Finally, cut the meat between the rib bones, and your meal is ready to be served!

Per serving:

Calories 829

Total fat 46g

Total carbs 4g

Protein 86g

Sodium: 181mg

121.   Pork Belly

Prepare it in: 30 minutes

Cook it in: 1 hour and 30 minutes

Servings: 4

Ingredients:

- Pork Belly (2 Lbs.)
- Black Pepper (1 T.)
- Butter (1 T.)

Instructions:

1. As you can already tell, pork belly is high in fat and high in calories. The good news is that you are on the carnivore diet, and none of that matters; bring on the pork belly! To start off, you are going to want to heat your oven to 400 degrees.

2. To prepare your pork belly, you are going to want to score the belly skin. You will want to be careful not to cut the meat during this step, so take your time. When this is completed, go ahead and rub on the salt and pepper. You can use as much or as little seasoning as you desire!

3. When you are ready, place the pork belly into a roasting pan and place into the oven for thirty minutes. After this time has passed, you will want to turn the heat down to 320 degrees and then roast it for another twenty-five minutes per half-pound of meat.

4. Once the pork belly has cooked through, you have the option to switch on the broiler for a few minutes. By doing this, you can achieve a nice, crispy skin to dig into!

5. When your meat is cooked to the desired temperature, you will want to carefully remove the dish from your oven. I suggest waiting thirty minutes or so to allow the flavors to fully form in your pork belly. After that, you can slice up the meat, and your meal is ready to be served!

Per serving:

Calories: 1,200

Fats: 120g

Proteins: 20g

122. Chipotle Rubbed Tri-Tip

Prepare it in: 30 minutes

Cook it in: 30 minutes

Servings: 4-6

Ingredients

- 1 beef tri-tip
- Extra virgin olive oil
- Your favorite salsa, for serving

For the rub:

- 1 tablespoon coarse salt (kosher or sea)
- 1-1/2 teaspoons Chipotle chili powder
- 1-1/2 teaspoons Oregano, preferably Mexican
- 1 teaspoon granulated garlic
- 1/2 teaspoon ground cumin
- 1/2 teaspoon freshly ground black pepper

Instructions:

1. Fire up your traeger grill to medium-high, preferably at about 225 degrees.

2. You could opt for mesquite or your favorite flavor of traegers.

3. Mix ingredients to make the rub in a small clean bowl, stir until it is well combined.

4. Ensure your hands are clean. Next, place the tri-tip in a baking dish and sprinkle rub all over the sides, using your fingers, pat the rub into the meat. Drizzle some amount of virgin olive oil over mixture and rub.

5. Next, transfer the tri-tip to the grill. Reduce the lid and grill the tri-tip until the grill heats up to 100 degrees. Grill for about one hour. Sometimes, it could take lesser time. Remove tri-tip from grill and place in a plate with a foil covering.

6. Heat grill again till about 600 degrees. When at 600 degrees, switch to Open Flame Cooking Mode. Carefully pull out the grill grates and the Hatch and replace with the Direct Flame Insert.

7. Extract the tri-tip from the foil. Place on sear. Sear the tri-tip until it reaches about 120 degrees. It would be crusty and browned on the outside and rare in the center; 130 degrees for medium-rare (or to taste). Cook the two sides for about 4 minutes, turning with thongs. Transfer the tri-tip to a board and cut.

8. Cool meat for about 2 minutes. With a knife make thin cuts across the grain. Top with your favorite salsa and enjoy.

Per serving:

Calories: 50

Carbohydrates: 4g

Fat: 8g

Protein: 7.6g

Fiber: 3.2g

123. Cheeseburger Hand Pies

Prepare it in: 35 minutes

Cook it in: 10 minutes

Servings: 6

Ingredients:

- ½ pound lean ground beef
- 1 tablespoon minced onion
- 1 tablespoon steak seasoning
- 1 cup cheese
- 8 slices white American cheese, divided
- 2 (14-ounce) refrigerated prepared pizza dough sheets, divided
- 2 eggs
- 24 hamburger dill pickle chips
- 2 tablespoons sesame seeds
- 6 slices tomato, for garnish
- Ketchup and mustard, for serving

Instructions:

1. Supply your smoker with wood pellets and follow the manufacturer's specific start-up procedure. Preheat, with the lid closed, to 325°F.

2. On your stove top, in a medium sauté pan over medium-high heat, brown the ground beef for 4 to 5 minutes, or until cooked

through. Add the minced onion and steak seasoning.

3. Toss in the shredded cheese blend and 2 slices of American cheese and stir until melted and fully incorporated.

4. Remove the cheeseburger mixture from the heat and set aside.

5. Make sure the dough is well chilled for easier handling. Working quickly, roll out one prepared pizza crust on parchment paper and brush with half of the egg wash.

6. Arrange the remaining 6 slices of American cheese on the dough to outline 6 hand pies.

Per serving:

Calories: 325

Fat: 21 g

Carbohydrates: 11 g

Protein: 23 g

Fiber: 0 g

124.   Pulled Beef

Prepare it in: 10 Minutes

Cook it in: 6 Hours

Servings: 6

Ingredients:

- 4 lb. beef sirloin tip roast
- 1/2 cup BBQ rub
- Two bottles of amber beer
- One bottle barbecues sauce

Instructions:

1. Turn your wood pellet grill onto smoke setting, then trim excess fat from the steak.

2. Coat the steak with BBQ rub and let it smoke on the grill for 1 hour.

3. Continue cooking and flipping the steak for the next 3 hours. Transfer the steak to a braising vessel. Add the beers.

4. Braise the beef until tender, then transfer to a platter reserving 2 cups of cooking liquid.

5. Use a pair of forks to shred the beef and return it to the pan. Add the reserved liquid and barbecue sauce. Stir well and keep warm

before serving.

6. Enjoy.

Per serving:

Calories 829

Total fat 46g

Total carbs 4g

Protein 86g

Sodium: 181mg

125. Grilled Veal with Mustard Lemony Crust

Prepare it in: 15 minutes

Cook it in: 2 hours and 45 minutes

Servings: 8

Ingredients

- 1 lb boneless veal leg round roast
- 1 tablespoon Dijon-style mustard
- 1 tablespoon lemon juice
- 1 teaspoon dried thyme, crushed
- 1 teaspoon dried basil, crushed
- 2 tablespoon water
- 1/2 teaspoon coarsely salt and ground pepper
- 1/4 cup breadcrumbs

Instructions:

1. Place meat on a rack in a shallow roasting pan.

2. In a small mixing bowl stir together bread crumbs, water, mustard, lemon juice, basil, thyme, and pepper. Spread the mixture over surface of the meat.

3. Start your traeger grill, set the temperature on High and preheat, lid closed, for 10 to 15 minutes.

4. As a general rule, you should grill steaks on high heat (450-500°F).

5. Grill about 7-10 minutes per side at high temperatures or 15-20 minutes per side at the lower temperatures, or to your preference for doneness.

6. Remove veal meat from the grill and let cool for 10 minutes.

Per serving:

Calories 172 cal

Fat 3g

Carbohydrates 4g

Fiber 0g

Protein 30g

126. Midnight Brisket

Prepare it in: 15 Minutes

Cook it in: 12 Minutes

Servings: 6

Ingredients:

- 1 tbsp Worcestershire sauce
- 1 tbsp Traeger beef Rub
- 1 tbsp Traeger Chicken rub
- 1 tbsp Traeger Blackened Saskatchewan rub
- 5 lb. flat cut brisket
- 1 cup beef broth

Instructions:

1. Rub the sauce and rubs in a mixing bowl, then rub the mixture on the meat.

2. Preheat your grill to 180°**F** with the lid closed for 15 minutes. You can use super smoke if you desire.

3. Place the meat on the grill and grill for 6 hours or until the internal temperature reaches 160°**F**.

4. Remove the meat from the grill and double wrap it with foil.

5. Add beef broth and return to grill, with the temperature increased to 225°**F**. **Cook for 4 hours or until the internal temperature reaches 204°F.**

6. Remove from grill and let rest for 30 minutes. Serve and enjoy with your favorite BBQ sauce.

Per serving:

Calories 200

Total fat 14g

Total carbs 3g

Protein 14g

Sodium: 680mg

127. Bacon-Swiss Cheesesteak Meatloaf

Prepare it in: 15 minutes

Cook it in: 2 hours

Servings: 8-10

Ingredients:

- 1 tablespoon canola oil
- 2 garlic cloves, finely chopped
- 1 medium onion, finely chopped
- 1 poblano chile, stemmed, seeded, and finely chopped
- 2 pounds extra-lean ground beef
- 2 tablespoons Montreal steak seasoning
- 1 tablespoon A.1. Steak Sauce
- ½ pound bacon, cooked and crumbled
- 2 cups shredded Swiss cheese
- 1 egg, beaten
- 2 cups breadcrumbs
- ½ cup Tiger Sauce

Instructions:

1. On your stove top, heat the canola oil in a medium sauté pan over medium-high heat. Add the garlic, onion, and poblano, and sauté for 3 to 5 minutes, or until the onion is just barely translucent.

2. Supply your smoker with wood pellets and follow the manufacturer's specific start-up procedure. Preheat, with the lid closed, to 225°F.

3. In a large bowl, combine the sautéed vegetables, ground beef, steak seasoning, steak sauce, bacon, Swiss cheese, egg, and breadcrumbs. Mix with your hands until well incorporated, then shape into a loaf.

4. Put the meatloaf in a cast iron skillet and place it on the grill. Insert meat thermometer inserted in the loaf reads 165°F.

5. Top with the meatloaf with the Tiger Sauce, remove from the grill, and let rest for about 10 minutes before serving.

Per serving:

Calories: 120

Fat: 2 g

Carbohydrates: 0 g

Protein: 23 g

Fiber: 0 g

128.   London Broil

Prepare it in: 20 minutes

Cook it in: 12-16 minutes

Servings: 3-4

Ingredients:

- 1 (1½- to 2-pound) London broil or top round steak
- ¼ cup soy sauce
- 2 tablespoons white wine
- 2 tablespoons extra-virgin olive oil
- ¼ cup chopped scallions
- 2 tablespoons packed brown sugar
- 2 garlic cloves, minced
- 2 teaspoons red pepper flakes
- 1 teaspoon freshly ground black pepper

Instructions:

1. Using a meat mallet, pound the steak lightly all over on both sides to break down its fibers and tenderize. You are not trying to pound down the thickness.
2. In a medium bowl, make the marinade by combining the soy sauce, white wine, olive oil, scallions, brown sugar, garlic, red pepper flakes, and black pepper.
3. Put the steak in a shallow plastic container with a lid and pour the marinade over the meat. Cover and refrigerate for 4 hours.
4. Supply your smoker with wood pellets and follow the manufacturer's specific start-up procedure. Preheat, with the lid closed, to 350°F.
5. Place the steak directly on the grill, close the lid, and smoke for 6 minutes. Flip, then smoke with the lid closed for 6 to 10 minutes more, or until a meat thermometer inserted in the meat reads 130°F for medium-rare.
6. The meat's temperature will rise by about 5 degrees while it rests.

Per serving:

Calories: 316 Cal

Fat: 3 g

Carbohydrates: 0 g

Protein: 54 g

Fiber: 0 g

129. French Onion Burgers

Prepare it in: 35 minutes

Cook it in: 20-25 minutes

Servings: 4

Ingredients:

- 1-pound lean ground beef
- 1 tablespoon minced garlic
- 1 teaspoon Better Than Bouillon Beef Base
- 1 teaspoon dried chives
- 1 teaspoon freshly ground black pepper
- 8 slices Gruyere cheese, divided
- ½ cup soy sauce
- 1 tablespoon extra-virgin olive oil
- 1 teaspoon liquid smoke
- 3 medium onions, cut into thick slices (do not separate the rings)
- 1 loaf French bread, cut into 8 slices
- 4 slices provolone cheese

Instructions:

1. In a large bowl, mix together the ground beef, minced garlic, beef base, chives, and pepper until well blended.

2. Divide the meat mixture and shape into 8 thin burger patties.

3. Top each of 4 patties with one slice of Gruyere, then top with the remaining 4 patties to create 4 stuffed burgers.

4. Supply your smoker with wood pellets and follow the manufacturer's specific start-up procedure. Preheat, with the lid closed, to 425°F.

5. Arrange the burgers directly on one side of the grill, close the lid, and smoke for 10 minutes. Flip and smoke with the lid closed for 10 to 15 minutes more, or until a meat thermometer inserted in the burgers reads 160°F. Add another Gruyère slice to the burgers during the last 5 minutes of smoking to melt.

6. Meanwhile, in a small bowl, combine the soy sauce, olive oil,

and liquid smoke.

7. Arrange the onion slices on the grill and paste on both sides with the soy sauce mixture. Smoke with the lid closed for 20 minutes, flipping halfway through.

8. Lightly toast the French bread slices on the grill. Layer each of 4 slices with a burger patty, a slice of provolone cheese, and some of the smoked onions. Top each with another slice of toasted French bread. Serve immediately.

Per serving:

Calories: 704

Fat: 43 g

Carbohydrates: 28 g

Protein: 49 g

Fiber: 2 g

130. Cocoa Crusted Grilled Flank Steak

Prepare it in: 15 Minutes

Cook it in: 6 Minutes

Servings: 7

Ingredients:

- 1 tbsp cocoa powder
- 2 tbsp chili powder
- 1 tbsp chipotle chili powder
- 1/2 tbsp garlic powder
- 1/2 tbsp onion powder
- 1-1/2 tbsp brown sugar
- 1 tbsp cumin
- 1 tbsp smoked paprika
- 1 tbsp kosher salt
- 1/2 tbsp black pepper
- Olive oil
- 4 lb. Flank steak

Instructions:

1. Whisk together cocoa, chili powder, garlic powder, onion powder, sugar, cumin, paprika, salt, and pepper in a mixing bowl.

2. Drizzle the steak with oil, then rub with the cocoa mixture on both sides.

3. Preheat your wood pellet grill for 15 minutes with the lid closed.

4. Cook the meat on the grill grate for 5 minutes or until the internal

temperature reaches 135**°F.**

5. Remove the meat from the grill and cool for 15 minutes to allow the juices to redistribute.

6. Slice the meat against the grain and on a sharp diagonal.

7. Serve and enjoy.

Per serving:

Calories 420

Total fat 26g

Total carbs 21g

Protein 3g

Sugar 7g,

Fiber 8g

Sodium: 2410mg

131. Grill Prime Rib Roast

Prepare it in: 5 Minutes

Cook it in: 4 Hours

Servings: 10

Ingredients:

- 7 lb. bone prime rib roast
- Traeger prime rib rub

Instructions:

1. Coat the roast generously with the rub, then wrap in a plastic wrap. Let sit in the fridge for 24 hours to marinate.

2. Set the temperatures to 500°F.to to preheat with the lid closed for 15 minutes.

3. Place the rib directly on the grill fat side up and cook for 30 minutes.

4. Decrease the temperature to 300°F and cook for 4 hours or until the internal temperature is 120°F- rare, 130°F-medium rare, 140°F-medium and 150°F-well done.

5. Remove from the grill and let rest for 30 minutes, then serve and enjoy.

Per serving:

Calories 290

Total fat 23g

Total carbs 0g

Protein 19g

Sodium: 54mg

Potassium 275mg

132.   Corned Beef and Cabbage

Prepare it in: 30 minutes

Cook it in: 4-5 hours

Servings: 6-8

Ingredients:

- 1-gallon water
- 1 (3- to 4-pound) point cut corned beef brisket with pickling spice packet
- 1 tablespoon freshly ground black pepper
- 1 tablespoon garlic powder
- ½ cup molasses
- 1 teaspoon ground mustard
- 1 head green cabbage
- 4 tablespoons (½ stick) butter
- 2 tablespoons rendered bacon fat
- 1 chicken bouillon cube, crushed

Instructions:

1. Refrigerate overnight, changing the water as often as you remember to do so—ideally, every 3 hours while you're awake—to soak out some of the curing salt initially added.

2. Supply your smoker with wood pellets and follow the manufacturer's specific start-up procedure. Preheat, with the lid closed, to 275°F.

3. Remove the meat from the brining liquid, pat it dry, and generously rub with the black pepper and garlic powder.

4. Put the seasoned corned beef directly on the grill, fat-side up, close the lid, and grill for 2 hours. Remove from the grill when done.

5. In a small bowl, combine the molasses and ground mustard and pour half of this mixture into the bottom of a disposable aluminum pan.

6. Transfer the meat to the pan, fat-side up, and pour the remaining molasses mixture on top, spreading it evenly over the meat. Cover tightly with aluminum foil.

7. Transfer the pan to the grill, close

the lid, and continue smoking the corned beef for 2 to 3 hours, or until a meat thermometer inserted in the thickest part reads 185°F.

8. Rest meat Serve.

Per serving:

Calories: 295

Fat: 17 g

Carbohydrates: 19 g

Protein: 18 g

Fiber: 6 g

133. Grill Deli-Style Roast Beef

Prepare it in: 15 Minutes

Cook it in: 4 Hours

Servings: 2

Ingredients:

- 4lb round-bottomed roast
- 1 tbsp coconut oil
- 1/4 tbsp garlic powder
- 1/4 tbsp onion powder
- 1/4 tbsp thyme
- 1/4 tbsp oregano
- 1/2 tbsp paprika
- 1/2 tbsp salt
- 1/2 tbsp black pepper

Instructions:

1. Combine all the dry hubs to get a dry rub.

2. Roll the roast in oil, then coat with the rub.

3. Set your grill to 185°F and place the roast on the grill.

4. Smoke for 4 hours or until the internal temperature reaches 140°F.

5. Remove the roast from the grill and let rest for 10 minutes.

6. Slice thinly and serve.

Per serving:

Calories 90

Total fat 3g

Total Carbs 0g

Protein 14g

Sodium: 420mg

134. Longhorn Cowboy Tri-Tip

Prepare it in: 15 Minutes

Cook it in: 4 Hours

Servings: 7

Ingredients:

3 lb. tri-tip roast

1/8 cup coffee, ground

1/4 cup Traeger beef rub

Instructions:

1. Preheat the grill to 180°F with the lid closed for 15 minutes.

2. Meanwhile, rub the roast with coffee and beef rub. Place the roast on the grill grate and smoke for 3 hours.

3. Remove the roast from the grill and double wrap it with foil. Increase the temperature to 275°F.

4. Return the meat to the grill and cook for 90 minutes or until the internal temperature reaches 135°F.

5. Remove from the grill, unwrap it and let rest for 10 minutes before serving.

6. **Enjoy.**

Per serving:

Calories 245

Total fat 14g

Total Carbs 0g

Protein 23g

Sodium: 80mg

135.   Reverse Seared Flank Steak

Prepare it in: 10 Minutes

Cook it in: 10 Minutes

Servings: 2

Ingredients:

- 1.5 lb. Flanks steak
- 1 tbsp salt
- 1/2 onion powder
- 1/4 tbsp garlic powder
- 1/2 black pepper, coarsely ground

Instructions:

1. Preheat your wood pellet grill to 225°**F.**

2. In a mixing bowl, mix salt, onion powder, garlic powder, and pepper. Generously rub the steak

with the mixture.

3. Place the steaks on the preheated grill, close the lid, and let the steak cook.

4. Crank up the grill to high, then let it heat. The steak should be off the grill and tented with foil to keep it warm.

5. Once the grill is heated up to 450°F, place the steak back and grill for 3 minutes per side.

6. Remove from heat, pat with butter, and serve. Enjoy.

Per serving:

Calories 112

Total fat 5g

Total carbs 1g

Protein 16g

Sodium: 737mg

136.   Pastrami

Prepare it in: 10 minutes

Cook it in: 4-5 hours

Servings: 12

Ingredients:

- 1-gallon water, plus ½ cup

- ½ cup packed light brown sugar

- 1 (3- to 4-pound) point cut corned beef brisket with brine mix packet

- 2 tablespoons freshly ground black pepper

- ¼ cup ground coriander

Instructions:

1. Cover and refrigerate overnight, changing the water as often as you remember to do so—ideally, every 3 hours while you're awake—to soak out some of the curing salt originally added.

2. Supply your smoker with wood pellets and follow the manufacturer's specific start-up procedure. Preheat, with the lid closed, to 275°F.

3. In a small bowl, combine the black pepper and ground coriander to form a rub.

4. Drain the meat, pat it dry, and generously coat on all sides with the rub.

5. Place the corned beef directly on

the grill, fat-side up, close the lid, and smoke for 3 hours to 3 hours 30 minutes, or until a meat thermometer inserted in the thickest part reads 175°F to 185°F.

6. Add the corned beef, cover tightly with aluminum foil, and smoke on the grill with the lid closed for an additional 30 minutes to 1 hour.

7. Remove the meat

8. Refrigerate

Per serving:

Calories: 123 Cal

Fat: 4 g

Carbohydrates: 3 g

Protein: 16 g

Fiber: 0 g

137.   Grill Teriyaki Beef Jerky

Prepare it in: 15 Minutes

Cook it in: 5 Hours

Servings: 10

Ingredients:

- 3 cups soy sauce
- 2 cups brown sugar
- Three garlic cloves
- 2-inch ginger knob, peeled and chopped
- 1 tbsp sesame oil
- 4 lb. beef, skirt steak

Instructions:

1. Place all the fixings except the meat in a food processor. Pulse until well mixed.

2. Trim any extra fat from the meat and slice into 1/4-inch slices. Add the steak with the marinade into a zip lock bag and let marinate for 12-24 hours in a fridge.

3. Set the wood pellet grill to smoke and let preheat for 5 minutes.

4. Arrange the steaks on the grill, leaving a space between each. Let smoke for 5 hours.

5. Remove the steak from the grill and serve when warm.

Per serving:

Calories 80

Total fat 1g

Total Carbs 7g

Protein 11g

Sugar 6g

Sodium: 390mg

138.   Grilled Butter Basted Rib-eye

Prepare it in: 20 Minutes

Cook it in: 20 Minutes

Servings: 4

Ingredients:

- Two rib-eye steaks, bone-in
- Salt to taste
- Pepper to taste
- 4 tbsp butter, unsalted

Instructions:

1. Mix steak, salt, and pepper in a Ziplock bag. Seal the bag and mix until the beef is well coated. Ensure you get as much air as possible from the Ziplock bag.

2. Set the wood pellet grill temperature to high with a closed lid for 15 minutes. Place a cast-iron into the grill.

3. Place the steaks on the grill's hottest spot and cook for 5 minutes with the lid closed.

4. Open the lid and add butter to the skillet. When it's almost melted, place the steak on the skillet with the grilled side up.

5. Cook for 5 minutes while busting the meat with butter. Close the lid and cook until the temperature is 130°**F.**

6. Remove the steak from the skillet and let rest for 10 minutes before enjoying with the reserved butter.

Per serving:

Calories 745

Total fat 65g

Total Carbs 5g

Net Carbs 5g

Protein 35g

139.   Supper Beef Roast

Prepare it in: 5 Minutes

144

Cook it in: 3 Hours

Servings: 7

Ingredients:

- 3-1/2 beef top round
- 3 tbsp vegetable oil
- Prime rib rub
- 2 cups beef broth
- One russet potato, peeled and sliced
- Two carrots, peeled and sliced
- Two celery stalks, chopped
- One onion, sliced
- Two thyme sprigs

Instructions:

1. Rub the roast with vegetable oil and place it on the roasting fat side up. Season with prime rib rub, then pours the beef broth.

2. Set the temperature to 500°F and preheat the wood pellet grill for 15 minutes with the lid closed.

3. Cook for 30 minutes or until the roast is well seared.

4. Reduce temperature to 225°F. Add the veggies and thyme and cover with foil. Cook for three more hours or until the internal temperature reaches 135°F.

5. Remove from the grill and let rest for 10 minutes. Slice against the grain and serve with vegetables and the pan drippings.

6. Enjoy.

Per serving:

Calories 697

Total fat 10g

Total Carbs 127g

Protein 34g

Sugar 14g

Fiber 22g

Sodium: 3466mg

Potassium 2329mg

140. Beef Tenderloin with Balsamic Glaze

Prepare it in: 30 minutes

Cook it in: 10 minutes

Servings: 6

Ingredients

- Balsamic Reduction

- 3-4 tablespoons of butter
- 1/3 cups of brown sugar
- 3 tablespoons of fresh rosemary finely chopped
- 3 cups of balsamic vinegar
- 3 garlic cloves of peeled and crushed
- Salt and pepper
- Beef Tenderloin
- Remove silver skin from the trimmed meat

Instructions:

1. Cook the tail (chain portion) by folding it up to ensure an even grilling. Old, the tail together with toothpicks or a butcher's twine, then season with beef rub.

2. Pre-heat wooden traeger smoker grill to about 250 degrees F. At the bottom of the rack, cook the meat for about sixty minutes. Keep an eye on the loins. Let the tender loins reach an average temperature of 115 degrees.

3. Extract the meat from the grill and let cool off. The next thing is to increase the grill heat to about 500 degrees F to sear. Once this is done, place the meat on the searing rack and sear each side for about a minute.

4. The final temperature of the dish should be about 130 degrees. Extract tenderloin from the grill and allow cooling off on a cutting board. With a sharp chef knife, slice the meat into strips. Take the balsamic reduction and drizzle over meat to get the final product.

Per serving:

Calories: 40 cal

Carbohydrates: 0g

Fat: 3g

Protein: 8g

Fiber: 0g

Sweets and Desserts

141. Peppermint Chocolate Chip Cookies

Prepare it in: *10 minutes*

Cook it in: *40 minutes*

Servings: *3*

Ingredients

- 1 cup butter, softened
- 1 cup white sugar
- ½ cup light brown sugar
- 2 eggs
- 2 teaspoons peppermint extract
- 1 teaspoon pure vanilla extract
- 2 cups flour
- ½ cup dark cocoa powder
- baking soda (1 teaspoon)
- 1 teaspoon baking powder
- ¼ teaspoon salt
- 1 cup white chocolate chips
- 1 cup crushed candy cane pieces

Instructions

1. In a large bowl, combine the butter, white sugar, and brown sugar. Using an electric mixer, blend the ingredients until creamy.

2. Next, add in the eggs, peppermint extract, and vanilla extract and mix until blended.

3. In a separate bowl, sift together the flour, cocoa powder, baking soda, baking powder, and salt.

4. Working in increments, mix the dry ingredients into the wet ingredients.

5. Add the white chocolate chips and crushed candy cane pieces into the bowl and fold in until the chips are worked evenly throughout the dough.

6. Cover the dough with plastic wrap and refrigerate for at least 2 hours.

7. Remove the dough from the refrigerator and preheat the oven to 350°F.

8. Using your hands, form the dough into balls measuring approximately 1 inch in diameter.

9. Place the balls on an ungreased baking sheet and then place the baking sheet in the oven.

10. Bake for 10-12 minutes or until done.

Per serving:

Calories 290

Total fat 23g

Total carbs 0g

Protein 19g

Sodium: 54mg

Potassium 275mg

142. Christmassy Hedgehog Slices

Prepare it in: *10 minutes*

Cook it in: *60 minutes*

Servings: *8*

Ingredients

- ½ cup butter
- 1 8 ounce/250 g package shortbread cookies such as

Scotch finger biscuits

- 1 teaspoon vanilla extract
- ⅔ cup white sugar
- ½ cup dry cranberries
- ½ cup pecans or almonds
- ½ cup tablespoons coconut flakes
- 2 tablespoons baking cocoa
- 1 cup semi-sweet chocolate chips
- 1 can of sweetened condensed milk (14 ounces/300 g)
- Cooking spray

Instructions

1. Line the bottom of an 8" round cake pan with wax paper or parchment paper. Grease the pan side and paper liner bottom with cooking spray.

2. In a saucepan, over medium heat, melt the chocolate chips with the condensed milk and butter, about 4-5 minutes, stirring occasionally with a wooden spoon. Remove from the heat, and let it cool down for a few minutes.

3. Crumble the cookies in small pieces, about the size of hazelnuts

or peas, in a large mixing bowl.

4. Add the coconut, pecans, cranberries, and cocoa. Stir a few times to combine.

5. Pour the chocolate mixture into the mixing bowl with the dry ingredients. Stir until all the ingredients are well coated.

Per serving:

Calories: 145

Fat: 9.4g

Saturated Fat: 4.6g

Trans Fat: 4.8g

Carbohydrates: 1g

Fiber: 0.1g

Sodium: 1200mg

Protein: 14.3g

143.   Fruitcake Cookies

Prepare it in: *10 minutes*

Cook it in: *40 minutes*

Servings: 7

Ingredients

- 1 cup butter, softened
- 1 cup powdered sugar
- 1 egg
- 1 teaspoon pure vanilla extract
- 1 tablespoon bourbon
- 2 ¼ cup flour, sifted
- ¼ cup candied ginger, chopped
- 1 cup pecans, chopped
- 1 ½ cup dried or candied fruit assortment (cherries, pineapple, apricots, etc), chopped

Instructions

1. Using an electric mixer, combine the softened butter and powdered sugar until creamy.

2. Add in the egg, vanilla extract, and bourbon. Continue mixing until blended.

3. Working in increments, add in the sifted flour just until blended.

4. Add the pecans, candied ginger, and dried or candied fruit to the bowl. Using a spoon, mix until the nuts and fruits are worked in evenly throughout the dough.

5. Cover the dough with plastic wrap and place in the refrigerator

for 1 hour.

6. Remove the dough from the refrigerator and divide it into three equal sections.

7. Roll each section into a log and wrap it securely with plastic wrap. Place the logs back into the refrigerator for at least two hours or overnight.

8. Remove the cookie logs from the refrigerator and preheat the oven to 325°F.

9. Unwrap the logs and slice the dough into pieces that are approximately ¼ inch thick.

10. Place the cookies on an ungreased baking sheet, making sure to leave at least ½ to 1 inch between them.

11. Place the cookie sheet in the oven and bake for 12-15 minutes, or until the cookies turn a light golden brown and the edges begin to crisp.

Per serving:

Calories: 434

Fat: 35.3g

Carbs: 10.5g

Protein: 18.4g

144.   Kiss Sugar Cookies

Prepare it in: *10 minutes*

Cook it in: *40 minutes*

Servings: *3*

Ingredients

- 48 chocolate Kisses, of the flavor of your choice, I like peppermint for the holidays
- ½ cup butter, at room temperature
- 1 cup white sugar
- 1 large egg
- 1½ teaspoons vanilla extract
- 2 cups all-purpose flour
- ¼ teaspoon baking soda
- ¼ teaspoon salt
- 2 tablespoons milk
- Red or green sugar crystals

Instructions

1. Preheat the oven to 350°F and

place the oven rack in the middle position.

2. Unwrap the chocolate kisses and set them aside.

3. With an electric mixer, cream the butter and sugar on high speed until fluffy, about 2-3 minutes.

4. Add the sugar, vanilla, and egg, and beat until well mixed.

5. Combine flour, baking soda, and salt. Stir until well mixed.

6. Add gradually the flour mix with the butter mixture. Add the milk. Beat until the cookie dough is light and smooth.

7. Place colored sugar crystals in a shallow dish.

8. Form 1" balls with the palm of your hands. Drop the formed cookie balls in the colored sugar and cover it with the sugar.

9. Place the prepared cookie on an ungreased cookie sheet lined with parchment paper.

10. Bake for 8 to 10 minutes or till the edges of the cookies become golden brown.

11. Remove from the oven. Let cool for a few minutes.

12. Place a candy in the middle of each cookie.

13. Place the cookies on a wire rack with a spatula. Allow to cool down completely, about 20-30 minutes.

Per serving:

Calories: 145

Fat: 9.4g

Saturated Fat: 4.6g

Trans Fat: 4.8g

Carbohydrates: 1g

Fiber: 0.1g

Sodium: 1200mg

Protein: 14.3g

145. Christmas Tree Meringue Cookies

Prepare it in: *10 minutes*

Cook it in: *40 minutes*

Servings: 3

Ingredients

- 4 large egg whites
- 1⅓ cups superfine sugar
- ¼ teaspoon cream of tartar
- ¼ teaspoon salt
- ¼ teaspoon peppermint extract (optional)
- Green food coloring (gel is preferred, and just a little is needed))
- Green gel writing frosting (optional)
- 1 ounce of semi-sweet chocolate (optional)
- Material
- Piping bag with a star fitting tip
- Cookie sheet lined with parchment paper
- Large clean cookie sheet for the chocolate star

Instructions

1. Preheat the oven to 150°F, and place the oven rack in the middle position.
2. Beat the egg whites on high speed until foamy and white.
3. Add the cream of tartar, the salt, and the peppermint extract if desired. Continue beating at high speed until soft peaks form.
4. Add the sugar very, very slowly as the mixer continues to beat the egg white mixture at medium-low speed. It should take exactly 7 minutes. This step is important. It will make your meringue light and fluffy. It can be useful to set a timer so as not to lose track of the time you need to incorporate the sugar.
5. Add a few drops of green food coloring, and mix it in with a spatula or wooden spoon until you get the desired color shade.
6. Place the meringue mixture in a piping bag already set with a star-shaped tip.
7. Cut some parchment paper to fit the bottom of a large cookie sheet.
8. Pipe the meringue in a continuous movement to shape small Christmas trees with a

pointing tip finish, about 1" apart from each other.

9. Bake for 2 hours to 2½ hours until the meringue cookies are dry and crispy.

10. Check often on the meringue cookies after 1¾ hours so they do not start to brown.

11. Remove from the oven. Let cool on a wire rack.

12. To make the chocolate star for the treetop, place a cookie sheet in the freezer for 10 to 15 minutes until it is very cold.

13. Reverse the cookie sheet on your working surface so the bottom is facing you.

14. Melt the chocolate in the microwave for about 30 seconds, until it's all melted but not burned. Let it cool down for about 2 minutes.

15. Place the melted chocolate in a fabric piping bag set with the smallest round tip.

16. Draw in one movement the star shape on the back of the cold cookie sheet. Make as many as you have meringue for.

17. Wait until the chocolate star is completely cooled down to remove them delicately with a spatula.

18. Carefully glue a star onto each meringue treetop with the green writing gel frosting. Add some gel frosting on the Christmas tree if desired to create shade.

19. Sprinkle it with powdered sugar to imitate snow.

Per serving:

Calories 290

Total fat 23g

Total carbs 0g

Protein 19g

Sodium: 54mg

Potassium 275mg

146.   Sweet Belgium

Prepare it in: 10 minutes

Cook it in: 50 minutes

Servings: 3

Ingredients

- 1 cup Date Caramel
- 5½ ounces chocolate salami (or dark chocolate)
- 5 ounces Fromage de Bruxelles (or any soft cow milk cheese, or double-cream brie)
- 4 hazelnut croissants (or plain croissants spread with Nutella)
- 4 plain croissants
- 1 cup raspberries
- 2 cups strawberries
- You will also need: a large board, a small knife, a small bowl, a small spoon, a cheese knife

Instructions

1. Prepare the date caramel spread according to the recipe. If necessary, this can be made up to 3 days ahead of time, but it's best served fresh.

2. Slice half of the chocolate salami into thin rounds. Place the slices and the remaining large piece in the bottom right corner of the board. Put a small knife next to it.

3. In the center of the board, place the Fromage de Bruxelles with a cheese knife.

4. Put the date caramel spread in a small bowl with a spoon and place it in the top right corner of the board with a small spoon in the bowl.

5. Stack the croissants along the left side of the board.

6. Scatter the raspberries on the Fromage, cascading down one side.

7. Fill in the blank spaces around the date caramel bowl with the strawberries.

Drink pairing: An espresso martini is an invigorating drink to accompany this board. To make one, combine 2 ounces vodka (we like White Nights Vodka from Belgium), ½ ounce simple syrup, ½ ounce coffee liqueur, and 1 ounce chilled brewed espresso in a cocktail shaker filled with ice.

Shake well, then strain into a martini glass garnished with a rim of chocolate sprinkles.

Per serving:

Calories: 145

Fat: 9.4g

Saturated Fat: 4.6g

Trans Fat: 4.8g

Carbohydrates: 1g

Fiber: 0.1g

Sodium: 1200mg

Protein: 14.3g

147.   Brandied Christmas Cut-Outs

Prepare it in: *10 minutes*

Cook it in: *40 minutes*

Servings: *3*

Ingredients

- 1 cup butter, softened
- 1 ½ cup sugar
- 2 eggs
- 1 tablespoon plus 2 teaspoons good quality brandy
- 1 teaspoon pure vanilla extract
- 3 cups flour
- ½ cup pecans, finely ground
- ½ teaspoon cinnamon
- ½ teaspoon ground ginger
- ½ teaspoon nutmeg
- ¼ teaspoon salt

Instructions

1. In a large bowl, combine the butter and sugar. Using an electric mixer, blend the ingredients until creamy.

2. Next, add the eggs, brandy, and vanilla extract and mix until blended.

3. In a separate bowl, sift together the flour, cinnamon, ginger, nutmeg, salt, and finely ground pecans.

4. Working in increments, add the dry ingredients into the wet and mix until blended.

5. Cover the dough tightly with plastic wrap and place the dough in the refrigerator for at least 2 hours or overnight.

6. Remove the dough from the refrigerator and preheat the oven to 400°F.

7. Lightly dust a countertop with flour and roll the dough out into approximately ¼ inch thickness.

8. Using your choice of cookie cutters, cut the cookies out into circles or festive shapes and then place them on an ungreased cookie sheet.

9. Place the cookie sheet in the oven and bake for 10-12 minutes, or until golden brown.

Per serving:

Calories 290

Total fat 23g

Total carbs 0g

Protein 19g

Sodium: 54mg

Potassium 275mg

148.   Holiday Spice Cutout Cookies

Prepare it in: 10 minutes

Cook it in: 10 minutes

Servings: 3

Ingredients

Dough

- ¼ cup unsalted butter (softened)
- ¾ cup sugar
- ¼ cup apple sauce
- ¾ cup molasses
- 1 egg
- 3 tablespoons fat-free milk
- 3¾ cups all-purpose flour
- 1 teaspoon ground ginger
- 2 teaspoons ground cinnamon
- 1 teaspoon ground aniseed
- 1 teaspoon ground cloves
- baking soda (1 teaspoon)

Frosting

- 4 to 5 tablespoons milk
- 5 cups sugar (confectioner's)
- ½ teaspoon pure vanilla extract
- ¼ cup unsalted butter (softened)
- Colored sugar crystal or sprinkles, for decoration, if desired

Instructions

1. In the large mixing bowl of the

electric mixer, cream the butter and sugar until pale yellow and fluffy.

2. Beat the apple sauce, molasses, egg, and milk for about 2 minutes.

3. Stir together the flour, cinnamon, ginger, aniseed, cloves, and baking soda in a mixing bowl. Mix well.

4. Add the dry ingredients to the creamed mixture. Beat until you obtain a smooth dough. Cut in 2, and cover each dough half with plastic wrap. Refrigerate for at least 2 hours until the dough is firm.

5. While the dough is resting in the refrigerator, prepare the frosting. Beat the butter and sugar with an electric mixer set on high speed until light and creamy. Beat in vanilla and enough milk to achieve a light and fluffy consistency.

6. If you want colored frosting, separate the frosting in a little plastic container and add a tiny bit of food coloring of your chosen color. Mix well. Add more food coloring if required to have the color you want. Again, I use food coloring paste as the colors are more vivid and it takes so little.

7. Cover the frosting in airtight containers until ready to use.

8. Lightly sprinkle some flour on a clean working surface. Using a rolling pin, roll out one of the cookie dough halves to ¼". Keep the second half of the dough in the refrigerator until you are ready to use it.

9. Cut the cookies out with Christmas-shaped cookie cutters.

10. If the cookies are to be used as decorations for the Christmas tree, make a hole using a plastic straw, set at least ¼" inch from the edge of the cookie top.

11. Place 1" apart on parchment-lined baking pans that haven't

been greased. Preheat oven to 375°F and bake for 8-10 minutes, or until golden brown around the edges. Remove the cookies from the oven and cool completely before icing.

Per serving:

Calories: 145

Fat: 9.4g

Saturated Fat: 4.6g

Trans Fat: 4.8g

Carbohydrates: 1g

Fiber: 0.1g

Sodium: 1200mg

Protein: 14.3g

149.   Snow Ball Cookies

Prepare it in: *10 minutes*

Cook it in: *40 minutes*

Servings: 5

Ingredients

- 2 cups pecans
- 1 cup butter, at room temperature
- 1¼ cup powdered sugar, and more if required
- 2 cups all-purpose flour

Instructions

1. Preheat the oven to 300ºF, and place the oven rack in the middle position.

2. Place the pecans in a food processor. Pulse until the nuts are all crushed finely.

3. In a mixing bowl, add the butter and ¼ cup of the powdered sugar. Beat on high until creamy, about 2 minutes.

4. Add the pecans to the butter mixture. Beat on low speed until just combined.

5. Add the flour gradually, and beat until well mixed.

6. You should get a thick batter.

7. Make about 48 balls of even size about ¾" to 1" in diameter. Take the time needed to roll well with the palms of your hands.

8. Place the balls on an ungreased cookie sheet, about ½" apart.

9. Place in the oven, and bake for 40 minutes.

10. Place the remaining powdered sugar in a shallow dish.

11. Roll the balls in the powdered sugar, while they are still hot but cooled enough to handle. Place on a waxed paper to rest.

12. Repeat a second time, rolling the snowball in the powdered sugar. Add some powdered sugar if needed.

13. Cool completely before placing in an airtight container, and refrigerate.

Per serving:

Calories: 145

Fat: 9.4g

Saturated Fat: 4.6g

Trans Fat: 4.8g

Carbohydrates: 1g

Fiber: 0.1g

Sodium: 1200mg

Protein: 14.3g

150. Butter Christmas Cookies

Prepare it in: *10 minutes*

Cook it in: *40 minutes*

Servings: *3*

Ingredients

- 1 cup butter, softened
- 3 ounces cream cheese, at room temperature
- ¾ cup white sugar
- 1 large egg
- 1 teaspoon pure vanilla extract
- 3 cups all-purpose flour
- Colored sugar crystal for decoration, red, green, and multicolored.

Instructions

1. In a mixing bowl, beat the butter and cream cheese with an electric mixer on high speed until light and fluffy, about 2 minutes. Add the sugar. When well mixed, put in the egg and vanilla. Beat until well mixed on medium speed, about 2 minutes.

2. Gradually add the flour by increments of half a cup. Beat at about medium speed until well combined and a ball of dough forms, about 4 minutes.

3. Split the dough in two. Wrap each half with plastic wrap.

4. Put in the refrigerator for about 2 hours or until the dough is firm.

5. Preheat the oven to 375°F and place the oven rack in the middle position.

6. Take one of the dough halves out of the refrigerator, and keep the other half in the refrigerator until you are ready to use it.

7. Lightly sprinkle some flour on a working surface. With a rolling pin, roll out the dough to about ¼" thick.

8. Using various Christmas-shaped cookie cutters, cut out the shapes.

9. Transfer the cookies to ungreased cookie sheets lined with parchment paper, leaving 1" between each cookie.

10. Sprinkle the cookies with red, green, or multi-colored sugars before baking.

11. Place in the oven, and bake for 7-9 minutes or until the edges are lightly golden brown. Remove from the oven.

12. Sprinkle the cookies with more colored crystal sugar while the cookies are still warm.

Per serving:

Calories: 145

Fat: 9.4g

Saturated Fat: 4.6g

Trans Fat: 4.8g

Carbohydrates: 1g

Fiber: 0.1g

Sodium: 1200mg

Protein: 14.3g

151.   Austrian Vanillekipferl Christmas Cookies

Prepare it in: 10 minutes
Cook it in: 40 minutes

Servings: 3

Ingredients

- 1 vanilla bean
- 14 tablespoons (1¾ sticks) unsalted butter
- 2 cups all-purpose flour
- ½ cup white sugar
- Powdered sugar
- 1 pinch salt
- 1 cup almond meal
- 3 egg yolks
- ½ teaspoon baking powder

Instructions

1. Split the vanilla bean lengthwise, and scrape the inside of the bean with a knife. Set aside.

2. In the large mixing bowl of the electric mixer, cream the butter, vanilla bean scrape, and white sugar on high speed until light and fluffy.

3. Add the almond meal, and beat until well mixed on medium speed.

4. Add the egg yolks, and beat until well mixed.

5. Combine the flour, baking soda, and salt in another mixing bowl. Stir well.

6. Add the dry ingredients to the creamed mixture. Beat on low speed until all the ingredients are just combined, and you have a smooth dough.

7. Split the dough into 4 pieces. Form a long roll shape with each of the 4 pieces of dough. Wrap in plastic wrap, and refrigerate for 2 hours until the dough is firm and very cold.

8. Preheat the oven to 350ºF, and place the oven rack in the middle position.

9. Cut pieces from the dough to form a cylinder of about ½" in diameter and 2½" in length. Make the extremities thinner and give the cookies a quarter-moon shape.

10. Place the cookies on an ungreased cookie sheet lined with parchment paper.

11. Bake for about 12 minutes, until the cookies' edges are becoming slightly golden.

12. Remove from the oven, and place the cookie sheet on a wire rack to cool down.

13. Place some powdered sugar in a shallow dish. When you can handle the cookies with your hand, roll the cookies in the powdered sugar twice.

14. Once they have completely cooled down, place the cookies in an airtight container. They will keep for up to a week...but they won't last that long!

Per serving:

Calories: 382

Fat: 29.1g

Saturated Fat: 4.5g

Trans Fat: 24.6g

Carbohydrates: 1.7g

Fiber: 0.1g

Sodium: 954mg

Protein: 25g

152.   Traditional Christmas Sugar Cookie

Prepare it in: *10 minutes*

Cook it in: *40 minutes*

Servings: *4*

Ingredients

Dough

- 1 ½ cups powdered sugar
- 1 cup butter, softened
- 1 teaspoon vanilla
- 1 egg
- 2½ cups all-purpose flour
- 1 teaspoon baking soda
- 1 teaspoon cream of tartar

Frosting

- 2 cups powdered sugar
- ½ teaspoon vanilla
- 2 tablespoons milk or half-and-half
- Food coloring, if desired
- Colored sugar crystal or sprinkles, if desired

Instructions

1. In a large mixing basin, beat powdered sugar, butter, vanilla, and egg with an electric mixer on medium speed until well combined. .

2. Add flour, baking soda, and cream of tartar. Mix until the dough becomes smooth, about 3-4 minutes.

3. Divide the dough into 2 balls, and wrap them in plastic wrap. Refrigerate for 3 hours or more, until the dough is firm.

4. While the cookie dough is resting, prepare the frosting. In a medium bowl, beat all frosting ingredients until smooth and fluffy on high speed for about 3-4 minutes.

5. If you want colored frosting, separate the frosting into little plastic containers, and add a tiny bit of food coloring of your chosen color. Mix well. Add more food coloring if required to have the color you want. I use food coloring paste as the colors are more vivid, and it takes so little.

6. Cover the frosting in airtight containers until ready to use.

7. Preheat the oven to 375°F and place the oven rack in the middle position.

8. Lightly sprinkle some flour on a clean working surface. Using a rolling pin, roll out one of the cookie doughs to ¼". Keep the second half of the dough in the refrigerator until you are ready to use it.

9. Cut the cookies out with Christmas-shaped cookie cutters.

10. If the cookies are to be used as decorations for the Christmas tree, make a hole using a plastic straw, set at least ¼" inch from the edge of the cookie top.

11. Transfer the cookies to an ungreased cookie sheet lined with parchment paper.

12. Place in the oven and bake for 7 to 8 minutes or until light brown. Remove from the oven, and let

the cookies cool down completely before frosting, about 30 minutes.

13. To frost the cookies, stir each frosting color with a spoon or small whisk until smooth. Place in a small plastic bag. Cut off a small piece of the bag's corner. Push out the frosting onto the cookie slowly. Frost and decorate cookies as desired with frosting and colored sugars.

Per serving:

Calories: 145

Fat: 9.4g

Saturated Fat: 4.6g

Trans Fat: 4.8g

Carbohydrates: 1g

Fiber: 0.1g

Sodium: 1200mg

Protein: 14.3g

153. Glazed Italian Christmas Cookies

Prepare it in: 10 minutes

Cook it in: 30 minutes

Servings: 3

Ingredients

- ½ cup butter
- 2 cups white sugar
- 4 large eggs
- 3 tablespoons baking powder
- 2 tablespoons pure vanilla extract
- 2 tablespoons pure almond extract
- 4 cups flour

Frosting

- 2 cup icing sugar
- ½ cup milk
- 1 teaspoon almond pure extract
- Food coloring, if desired
- Sugar sprinkle for decoration, if desired

Instructions

1. With an electric mixer, cream the butter and the sugar until smooth.

2. Add the eggs one by one, beating at medium speed.

3. Add the baking powder and vanilla and almond extract.

4. Gradually add the flour one cup at

a time. Mix until you have a ball of firm dough.

5. Split the dough in two, and form two balls. Wrap in plastic wrap, and chill dough in the refrigerator for 2 hours.

6. Preheat the oven to 375°F, and place the oven rack in the middle position.

7. Place one of the dough balls on a lightly floured surface. Roll out the dough to ¼" thick. Cut the cookies out using Christmas-shaped cookie cutters. Keep the second dough ball in the refrigerator until you are ready to use it.

8. Place the cutout cookies on ungreased cookie sheets lined with parchment paper.

9. Place in the preheated oven, and bake for 8-10 minutes, until the edges of the cookies start to brown.

10. Remove from the oven, and let the cookies rest for 10 minutes

before placing them on a wire rack. Let cool down completely before glazing them.

11. While the cookies are cooling down, you can prepare the glaze. In a small bowl, place the icing sugar. Add the almond extract and just enough milk to make a nice frosting consistency.

12. To glaze, dip the top of the cooled-down cookies into the glaze. Decorate with pearls or colored sugar or sprinkles.

Per serving:

Calories: 231

Fat: 8.4g

Saturated Fat: 4.6g

Trans Fat: 5.8g

Carbohydrates: 6g

Fiber: 0.1g

Sodium: 1300mg

Protein: 18.3g

154.   Classic Gingerbread Gentlemen

Prepare it in: *10 minutes*

Cook it in: *40 minutes*

Servings: *3*

Ingredients

- ⅓ cup butter or butter flavored shortening
- ½ cup dark molasses
- ¼ cup dark brown sugar
- ¼ cup white sugar
- 1 egg
- 2 cups flour
- 1 ½ teaspoon baking powder
- 2 tablespoons ginger powder
- 1 teaspoon cinnamon
- ½ teaspoon salt

Instructions

1. In a bowl combine the butter or butter-flavored shortening, molasses, brown sugar, and white sugar. Using an electric mixer, blend until creamy.

2. Add in the eggs and continue beating until blended.

3. In another bowl, sift together the flour, baking powder, ginger, cinnamon, and salt.

4. Working in increments, slowly add the dry ingredients into the wet ingredients, mixing just until blended.

5. Cover the dough and place it in the refrigerator for at least one hour or until firm.

6. Remove the dough from the refrigerator and preheat the oven to 375°F. Lightly grease or line a baking sheet.

7. Roll the dough out onto a lightly floured, flat surface.

8. Use gingerbread men cutouts that measure approximately 6 inches tall to cut out the shapes of the cookies.

9. Transfer the cookies to the prepared baking sheet and place it in the oven.

10. Bake for 10-12 minutes, or until the edges are nicely browned.

11. Cool on a baking rack and frost, if desired.

12. **Note:** If desired, you can decorate your gingerbread gentlemen with

nuts or candies before baking.

Per serving:

Calories 240

Fat 19g

Carbs 12g

Protein 15g

Conclusion

Charcuterie is not just meats and cheese, but includes all types of sauces and toppings such as jams, preserves, spreads, pickled items in jars or bottles, pates, cordons in jars or bottles or boxes in jars or bottles.

You'll find recipes for making all of the classics: bacon, salami, head cheese, salsas, bologna, pepperoni, chili and chili-lime sausage.

And there's even an entire chapter on making charcuterie for breakfast using ham and cheese sandwiches.

In some regions, charcuterie includes preserving fish using similar methods, to produce delicacies such as smoked salmon, lox, and pickled herring.

In today's world, the term has come to mean pairing preserved meats or seafood with cheeses, fruits, and many other accompaniments to serve at gatherings and celebrations. During get-togethers in our own home, charcuterie spreads serve as a focal point for family and friends to socialize and enjoy an abundance of flavors and textures from all over the world.

Charcuterie boards are not only gorgeous they contain a combination of flavor and nibbles for a simple no-fuss party snack

It's not difficult to prepare a cheese and meat board that everyone will rave about. Adding simple flavors from simple everyday ingredients takes very little prep and just a minute to build.

Made in the USA
Monee, IL
18 April 2022

7bbbe9a5-2fbf-4750-8013-179529993161R01